# Secrets of the Empowered Woman

## Create the Healthy Love and Life
## You Want and Deserve

**Sophia Rose, M.C.L.C.**

First Edition

ISBN: 978-0-578-36114-7

Wisdom Love Publishing, USA
Oceanside, California

TheLoveHealsMethod.com

*"Always remember that you are a unique and important person and that it is not selfish to love yourself."*

~ Dorothy C. Gresto

This book is dedicated to my courageous mother Dorothy who left this earth 35 years ago, but whose loving heart, fun-loving spirit, and beautiful soul will never be forgotten.

# ACKNOWLEDGEMENTS

To my mother, I still miss you, love you and wish you were here…thank you for being the inspiration for my life's work.

To my father, I love you, thank you for your love and support. I'm so grateful for the relationship we have shared in recent years.

To my sisters Donna and Adele and my brother Al, I love you all. To Adele thank you for your editing recommendations and suggestions.

To my nephew Albert, thank you for your love and technical support and to my niece Holly thank you for your love and interest in this book…I love you both.

To Cheryl Phillips, it's hard to express the gratitude I feel for all of the time, compassion, encouragement, help, and support that you have given me for so many years. Thank you for your incredible kindness, care, and generosity. Thank you for all of the reiki, for being my spiritual counselor and for always believing in me.

To Gail Braverman, thank you for your wise, kind-hearted generosity, support and compassion, for your very helpful insights about my life theme and for helping me through a very significant and challenging life transition.

To Michele Germain, thank you for all of the compassion, love and support that you have given to me over the years and through difficult times.

To my dear sweet friend and soul sister, Nancy Nelsen, thank you for coming back into my life, and for all of your love, support, and compassion. I'm so grateful for your friendship and support and the way we help each other through the ups and downs of our life journeys.

To my dear friend Autumn Stoff, thank you so much for your compassion, generosity, friendship, love, and support. Thank you for your encouragement, for believing in me and helping me when I really needed support.

To my sweet, soulmate ex-husband and ex-boyfriends, thank you for the love we shared and for all that I learned about love and relationships with you.

To Judith Balian, thank you for your patience, encouragement, kindness, support and generosity. Thank you very much for suggesting that I write this book and for all of your editing and publishing help. I couldn't have done it without you.

And lastly, thank you to all of my coaching clients and students who showed up over the years, and continue to show up to do the inner work on themselves, and who trusted me enough to share so honestly with me about their relationships, health, and lives. You have all touched my heart deeply and taught me so much.

–Sophia Rose

# TABLE OF CONTENTS

# INTRODUCTION

Congratulations! You're about to experience a new level of empowerment in your life! This book will change the way you show up as a woman in the world and how the world responds to you. What are the secrets to becoming a more empowered woman and how will this help you to create the healthy love and life you want and deserve? This book is my answer.

Over the past twenty years working as a teacher and coach in the holistic (body-mind-spirit) health and wellness field, I have seen that the state of a woman's health, life, and relationships are all interconnected. Eventually, I came to realize that what I was really teaching thousands of women—underneath the many details of why they came to me for support—was not just how to heal or transform their bodies, minds, hearts, and spirits. I was teaching them *how to love themselves and how to become more empowered women in their relationships and in their lives. This is what enabled them to manifest their healthy love and life dreams.*

Have you been struggling or settling for less than you want and deserve in your relationships or in other areas of your life? What if I told you that the answer to your challenges is *within you?* Would you like to know the secrets to creating the healthy love and life your heart desires? If so, this book is your guide. This is the resource and guide that I wish I had when I was a young woman. This is the book that I would love to see in the hands of every woman and the book that I would give to my own daughter if I had one. I offer it to you now, whatever your age or stage in life.

*This book is for every woman who has the courage to listen to her heart and follow her dreams in love and life.*

*May you come to know that your greatest power as a woman is love, starting with self-love and Divine Love--and that you are innately worthy of all that your heart desires.*

# THE FIVE KEY EMPOWERED WOMAN PRINCIPLES

One Saturday afternoon many years ago, I was pushing my shopping cart around the produce section in the natural grocery store, feeling so excited about seeing my boyfriend of three months for dinner later on that night. Yes, I had finally met "the one." We were so in love, and I was blissfully happy. Then I heard that exciting text ding on my cell phone, and I just knew it was him. I loved that sound and I loved getting his texts. I couldn't wait to see what he was going to say about dinner that night! I pushed my grocery cart full of organic produce over to the side of the aisle, took out my phone and read his text, "I won't be coming over for dinner tonight. Someone from my past has come back into my life and I have to see how it goes with her." That was it. It was over, or so I thought.

Completely shocked, physically shaken and heartbroken, I struggled to get through the checkout line without crying and then drove home in tears, overcome with grief, feeling completely abandoned, discarded, and rejected. How could this happen? Needless to say, my desire to understand healthy true love and what it meant to be an empowered woman became even more important to me after this painful experience. The on and off again relationship that I ended up having with this man for the next few years was a very significant relationship to me for several reasons, one of them being that it helped me to learn how to love myself and how to become a more empowered woman. For that I will always be grateful.

I'm here to tell you that you don't have to settle for crumbs in a romantic relationship or work for a boss who doesn't value and appreciate you. You don't have to settle for a job you dislike, or an unhealthy, unfulfilling relationship or life. You have the power to create the kind of healthy love and life that you desire. You are a very powerful woman. When you understand and learn the secrets to becoming a more empowered woman, instead of struggling or settling for less than you desire and deserve, you will begin the process of creating the healthy love and life that you've always wanted.

*Let's begin with the five key empowered woman principles and then continue with the seven empowered woman secrets.*

## KEY PRINCIPLE NUMBER ONE – YOU HAVE THREE RELATIONSHIPS

Whatever your relationship status, are you aware that you actually have three relationships, and that two of these relationships are *within you?* The *first relationship* that you have is with your Spiritual Source, or whatever name you choose to call the Divine—Spirit, Source, God, Goddess, Divine Love, Higher Power, The Universe, Divine Loving Intelligence, etc. You may not be aware of your relationship with a Spiritual Source; you may not give it much thought, time or attention; you might not even think of it as a relationship. But I have seen that most empowered women eventually come to understand the importance of having a relationship with their Spiritual Source and a deeper connection with their own heart and soul.

In chapter seven you will learn how to cultivate or strengthen your own unique personal relationship with your Spiritual Source and how practicing some form of meditation (or prayer) can help you become a more empowered woman in your relationships and in your life. For now, just know that your soul has a unique purpose for being here, a divine destiny to fulfill. *There is a divine loving power within you, beyond you, and all around you, and you live in a universe that wants to support you in fulfilling your deepest desires.*

The *second relationship* that you have is with yourself. I have noticed that most women are unaware of the fact that they have a relationship with themselves. I invite you to become very aware of the kind of relationship you have with yourself because *it is the foundation for all of your other relationships.* Other people, for example, will often treat you the way you treat yourself, and love you the way you love yourself. Your relationship with yourself is within you. ***As an empowered woman you have a very healthy, loving relationship with yourself.***

You are aware that there is a part of you, referred to as your inner child or your subconscious mind, that often holds hurts or false beliefs and may be in need of reparenting or subconscious mind reprogramming. At the same time, there is another part of you, often referred to as your soul or higher self, that knows the deeper truth about you and your life. I often refer to this part of you as your *Empowered Woman Within*. This empowered woman inside you can help you change your false beliefs, reparent your inner child, and change unhealthy behavior patterns that no longer serve you. You will learn about these two parts of yourself and about how to have a more loving relationship with yourself later in this book.

The *third kind of relationship* you have is of course the relationship that you have with other people, such as your partner or potential partners, your friends, your family, your co-workers, etc. These external relationships are what most people focus on, especially when there are challenges. As an empowered woman, I invite you to bring some of your attention and focus inside. I'm not saying that your external relationships aren't important. Of course having loving relationships with others is very important in life. I am saying that the more you concentrate on strengthening your two internal relationships, your relationship with your Spiritual Source and your relationship with yourself, the better your relationships with others will be and the more clarity you will have when you observe those around you and need to make important decisions.

***The bottom line is, the more loving your relationship is with yourself and the stronger your connection with your Spiritual Source, the less tolerance you will have for settling for less than you want and deserve, and the healthier and happier your relationships with other people and your life will be.***

## KEY PRINCIPLE NUMBER TWO – YOUR POWER IS WITHIN

*As an empowered woman you eventually come to realize that the ultimate source of your happiness is within you, and that the ultimate source of the peace and love that you seek on the outside is also within you.* This book will teach you the secrets to becoming a more empowered woman and how to create the healthy love and life you want *from the inside out,* because that is where your true power is—inside of you. *Your greatest power is LOVE, starting with self-love.*

*As an empowered woman you also know that any changes you want to make in your relationships or life need to start from within.* Most women focus only on trying to change the outer circumstances of their life to create what they want, while perhaps trying to think positive. But making changes from within involves more than your thinking and actions. It needs to also include changing *your energy* and *your feelings* because your emotions are even *more* powerful than your thoughts. Research has shown that your heart communicates more to your brain than your brain communicates to your heart!

As you awaken your *Empowered Woman Within*, you let go of trying to change, control or fix other people and situations you have no power over and stop feeling that other people and situations have power over you. *Instead, you learn how to love and empower yourself from within to create the healthy love and life you want and deserve.*

Please keep in mind that being a powerful woman does not mean that you'll never have any difficulties, losses, setbacks, or painful times and emotions, or that you always get everything you want when you want it. Being a powerful woman means that you have the internal strength to overcome adversity, pain, or challenges. And when you do, you rise up like the phoenix rising out of the ashes. *You rise up with grace, with an open, loving heart, and become even stronger and wiser than before, despite or even because of the difficult circumstances you have faced or that you may still be facing.*

Please also know that although you can *activate your full power* to create what you want in your life, *you are not in total control.* For example, you cannot control other people, their energies, their emotions and what they do in the world just as you cannot control Mother Nature and the weather. You can influence people who make important decisions and laws, but you cannot control the ultimate outcome. You may lose your home in a fire, lose your job in a pandemic, or get into a car accident because of a drunk driver. Things may happen that you didn't want or seek out. But this does not mean that you are helpless or powerless. You have a lot of power, even though you can't completely control or prevent painful things from happening to you or your loved ones. ***The good news is that you have the power within to intentionally create what you want, even while at the same time you are handling difficult or challenging circumstances in your life.***

*A helpful belief and attitude to have when going through difficult times is that everything happening in your life right now, no matter how challenging or painful, is ultimately happening to help you to grow in love and wisdom.* Everything is ultimately preparing you for your soul's purpose and destiny and the eventual fulfillment of your heart's desires. Learning how to perceive challenges from this higher perspective will be discussed further in chapters six and seven.

## KEY PRINCIPLE NUMBER THREE – EVERYTHING IS ENERGY

The secrets of the empowered woman journey that you are about to embark on follows the path of your body's seven major energy centers, commonly referred to as your *chakras*. These chakras, seen as spinning wheels of light in the deep center of your body, are very powerful energy centers where all four parts of you connect—*the physical, emotional, mental, and spiritual.* You will learn what it means to be in your power as a woman in each chakra and how they are all interconnected and work together.

***As an empowered woman, you understand the power of your energy. You understand that everything is energy.*** Your body is made up of energy, even though it appears to be solid. Your life force energy (your spirit), flows throughout your entire body and keeps you alive. Your emotions are energy; in fact, they are often referred to as energy in motion. Even though you can't see them, your thoughts and beliefs are energy. Your level of self-love, self-esteem, and self-confidence radiates energy out into your aura (the energy field around your body). Even though others may not consciously be aware of it, they can feel your energy. For example, if you say one thing but your energy is communicating something else, what people will feel and believe is your energy.

*Love is, of course, an energy. It is the most powerful and healing energy in the universe!* In relationships there is an exchange of energy between people. When you communicate, it's the energy that you're holding underneath your words that people feel and respond to. And when you want to heal, change something or create something new in your life, you definitely need to understand and become aware of your energy. Everything is energy, and as an empowered woman, you know that you must become the master of your own energy. *Learning how to make powerful shifts in your own energy is what will help you to create the healthy love and life that you want and deserve.*

Love, health, healing, and life transformation all start from within. Healing is about recognizing your innate wholeness. It is understanding that you have a body, you have feelings and emotions, as well as thoughts and beliefs, and you also have a soul and spirit—*and all of these parts of you are interconnected.*

## Your Energy System

In addition to having an immune system, a digestive system, and an endocrine system, etc., you also have an energy system. *The way that you make changes in yourself, your relationships or your life is by shifting your core energy with love.* Often, when you want to change something about yourself or your life, you need to become aware of the beliefs and emotions that have been stored in your energy system or in what is commonly referred to as your **subconscious mind.**

Below is a brief description of the three basic parts of your energy system. As you proceed with learning the seven secrets to becoming a more empowered woman, it will be helpful for you to become more aware of them.

**1. Your grounding cord**. Your grounding cord is like an energy meridian (energy meridians are where acupuncturists place their needles) that starts at the base of your spine and flows down into the earth. Everyone has one, even though you can't see it or may not be aware of it. Ideally it flows deep into the earth connecting you to the earth's supportive, stable, nourishing, and grounding energy. But very often, especially when you're experiencing a lot of stress or change, it can be challenging to feel grounded and connected to this powerful, supportive energy of the earth. As you will learn in chapter one, the first part of being an empowered woman is to be grounded and connected to the earth and your body, living fully in the present moment, not just up in your head, thinking about the future or the past.

**2. Your seven chakras** – Although you can't see them, your seven major chakras are spinning wheels of light in the deep center of your body near your spine. Each one is a different color of the rainbow. The first one is at the base of your spine. The second is in the center of your pelvis. The third is in your solar plexus area (between the bottom of your ribs and your navel). The fourth one is in your heart and chest area. The fifth one is in your throat. The sixth is in the center of your forehead, and the seventh is just touching the top of your head. If you've ever studied or practiced yoga, you're probably somewhat familiar with the chakras. If you're not familiar with them and this is the first time that you've heard of them, that's perfectly fine also. Each of the next seven chapters and seven secrets will correspond with one of these powerful chakras in your body.

**3. Your aura** - Everything that's going on and happening inside of you and within your chakras radiates out into your aura, which is the energy field around your body. A healthy aura usually radiates out about an arm's length from your body in all directions. As you learn to become a more empowered woman in all seven of your chakras, your energy will change in a very positive way and people will feel it.

*In order for you to stop struggling or settling in love and life, you may need to explore what's been holding you back and keeping you from stepping more fully into your true power and potential as a woman*. This often involves identifying and changing false beliefs and reprogramming emotional patterns in your subconscious mind that may be keeping you stuck in unfulfilling relationships or unpleasant repetitive life experiences. I invite you to start becoming aware of this as you read this book and move through each of the next seven chapters.

False beliefs and old, stuck, repetitive emotions create *energy blockages* in your body. You want your energy to flow freely, not to be stuck or blocked. Freeing yourself from these false beliefs and stuck emotions may involve reparenting your inner child or reprogramming the feelings and false beliefs you formed during your first seven years of your life. These feelings and false beliefs from the past will often get recreated in your adult life and relationships, as many of you have noticed, and can prevent you from being in your full power as a woman. *The good news is it's never too late to change old beliefs, feelings, and relationship patterns with love, starting with self-love. No matter what has happened in your past, tell yourself now that the best is yet to come!*

## KEY PRINCIPLE NUMBER FOUR – YOU HAVE BOTH MASCULINE AND FEMININE ENERGY

*Are you aware that you have both masculine and feminine energy?* Understanding the difference between these energies will not only help you to understand men better, but it will also help you to understand yourself better as a woman. You have both of these energies inside you, just as men do. It's really about finding the right balance for you between the two. And in a relationship with a partner, it's about finding out what feels more natural, enjoyable, and good to you. Every woman is different and unique.

*We all have varying degrees of masculine and feminine energy. In Chinese medicine, it's referred to as your yin and yang energy.* Although I sometimes use language for the heterosexual woman reader and heterosexual relationships in this book, the secrets and principles are equally applicable to other sexual orientations and same-sex relationships. This is because every human being (whatever their gender or sexual orientation), has a unique combination of yin and yang (feminine and masculine) energies within them. These energies also exist in the world around us with the sun and the moon, day and night, etc. As you read the following descriptions, you may want to ask yourself what feels more natural and like home to you? Do you feel more at home in one energy or the other, and at certain times or in certain situations? For example, on a date or with your partner you may enjoy and prefer to be more in your feminine energy, but at work perhaps you enjoy being more in your masculine energy.

*A very common problem I have seen over the years in my coaching practice is that many women have lost touch with or feel disconnected from their feminine energy because they have devalued and discounted it.* While deep down some women would like to be more in touch with it, especially if they have a feminine energy essence at their core, they may still find themselves in their masculine energy most of the time without being aware of it or knowing why. Many women even believe that the only way to be an empowered woman or have equality with men is to deny their feminine energy, emphasize their masculine energy, and "be more like a man."

One big reason for this is that for thousands of years our world has valued and emphasized masculine energy and discounted and devalued feminine energy. This is why we as women have often done the same thing to ourselves. You have likely devalued the beauty and power of your own feminine energy. You may have had to do so at times to be treated equally. Our society has taught both men and women to believe that feminine energy is weak, and that only masculine energy is strong. Nothing could be further from the truth.

*One reason why many people believe feminine energy is weak is because they grew up seeing weak role models of disempowered feminine energy or because they don't understand the difference between disempowered and empowered feminine energy. You'll be learning the difference shortly.* Empowered feminine energy is definitely not weak. The empowered masculine and empowered feminine energies that you have within you are very different, but they are equally as powerful. Depending on your natural core essence or your preference, you can choose at any time to be in one energy or the other or a combination of both. Because feminine energy has been devalued and discounted (in both men and women) for so many years, the emphasis in this book is on helping you to awaken and embrace your empowered feminine energy and to support it with your empowered masculine energy.

*Being an empowered woman means that you are your authentic true self, whatever that is for you. I believe that if you are discounting and devaluing any part of your authentic true self, then you are not in your power as a woman.*

The other equally common problem I see in my coaching practice that clearly relates to the first problem I just discussed, is women who grew up only learning from their mothers or other caretakers how to be in their *disempowered* feminine energy. This is also why I am emphasizing and teaching you in this book what it means to be in your *empowered* feminine energy and how to support it with your *empowered* masculine energy.

Let's take a look now at the differences between empowered and disempowered energies. As you read through the following explanations, please don't criticize yourself if you realize that you've been in your disempowered energies at times. It's all about awareness. Only when you become aware of something, can you make changes.

*Remember true healing and lasting transformation happens when you make changes with love.* All of us have fallen into disempowered energies at certain times or in certain relationships. The key is to become nonjudgmentally aware of it sooner rather than later, so that you can bring yourself back into your empowered energies with love. Let's begin by discussing *disempowered* feminine energy.

## Disempowered Feminine Energy

You're in disempowered feminine energy when you often feel like a victim, when you don't look at or take responsibility for your part in things, and you feel completely powerless to change anything in your life. In other words, when you're stuck in victim consciousness. You may have actually been victimized by someone or something at some point in your life, but that doesn't mean that you have to continue being a victim and have a victim mentality or consciousness, unless you choose to stay stuck and not make the changes you want to make in your relationships or life. At the same time, it's important to realize and accept that you are actually powerless to change certain things and to know the difference between what you truly have the power to change and what you don't. *You don't for example have the power to change other people, but you do absolutely have the power to change yourself.*

*A huge part of disempowered feminine energy is something that is often referred to as codependency.* Codependency is feeling and believing that other people are the ultimate source of your love, happiness, and self-worth. It's caring more about what other people think of you, instead of being true to yourself. Codependency is really a lack of self-love and self-worth. It's trying to get from others what you are not giving to yourself. It is being tuned in to everyone else's feelings and needs, but not your own. It's also taking on too much responsibility for other people's feelings which can result in your feeling inappropriate, unhealthy guilt.

*Codependency is a symptom of disempowered feminine energy.* This may involve being a people pleaser or excessive caretaking of others at the expense of your own health and well-being. Other clues that you may be codependent are taking on responsibility for others that is not yours and *having difficulty setting healthy boundaries.* Another sign is when you feel that you have to prove your worth or earn love because deep down you don't feel good enough and worthy just for who you are. Codependency is really a loss of connection to yourself, and staying connected to yourself is loving yourself. I will explain in chapters two and three what this means and why women sometimes develop these disempowering, codependent behaviors.

*Being emotionally reactive is also disempowered feminine energy.* It's when you're reacting from the little girl energy inside of you, rather than *responding* from your empowered woman self. You will learn more about responding versus reacting and mastering your emotions with secret two in chapter two. If you're in your disempowered feminine energy, you may also experience a lot of self-doubt, a lack of self-confidence, and possibly anxiety. This is because subconsciously, beneath many of your actions and behaviors, you're really seeking approval from others by trying to be perfect and prove your worth to earn people's love.

*Overall, when you're in your disempowered feminine energy, you are disconnected from your body, your feelings, your intuition, and your heart's desires. You may stay in relationships that are not fulfilling or healthy for you, out of guilt, fear of being alone, or concerns about not ever finding someone better.*

**Another sign of disempowered feminine energy is being passive or submissive.** You may allow yourself to be mistreated by others, and sometimes even abused, which happens when you don't have healthy boundaries. The interesting thing is that if you're in your *disempowered* feminine energy most of the time, you will often attract men or people who are in their *disempowered* masculine energy. **Masculine and feminine energies whether they are empowered or disempowered are attracted to each other like magnets.**

### Disempowered Masculine Energy

People with disempowered masculine energy may abuse power or try to *control, dominate or have power over others.* They often exhibit overly aggressive or passive-aggressive behavior. Someone in their disempowered masculine energy may also have *out-of-control* anger issues, lack discipline, and/or have addictions.

Disempowered masculine energy is overly competitive, it wants to win at any cost, rather than being competitive in a healthy way. It is also known to be unsupportive, critical, confrontational, disrespectful of boundaries, unstable, irresponsible, self-absorbed, and narcissistic. A person with disempowered masculine energy often has commitment issues, is emotionally unavailable, and doesn't want responsibility. They may use anger, blame, and projection to try to control or force an outcome. They may be defensive and often feel superior to women. Someone in their disempowered masculine energy may even use, exploit, or demean women due to a lack of respect and appreciation for feminine energy and women. Also, disempowered masculine energy gives but with an agenda; there is a "giving to get" something, which is manipulative.

If you've ever attracted and been in a relationship with someone who had some or many of the disempowered masculine energy characteristics just described, it may be because you have been in your disempowered feminine energy much of the time or because disempowered masculine energy is what you grew up with (perhaps with your father). If that's the case, that's what feels *familiar* to you. ***What you need to do to attract men or people who are in their empowered masculine energy is to reparent the little girl inside of you or reprogram your subconscious mind, and learn about what it means to be in your empowered feminine energy while supporting it with your own empowered masculine energy. You'll be learning how to do all of these things in this book.***

**Empowered Feminine Energy**

***Empowered feminine energy is about being in the present moment. It's being aware of what's happening within you and around you. It's being very much in tune with your body, feelings, emotional needs, your heart's desires, and your intuition.*** In fact, it's about "being" versus "doing." It's being receptive and able to receive from others. Your empowered feminine energy is about your emotions and the expression of them. It is also *trusting and allowing* things to unfold in your life as they are meant to. You're trusting your journey; you're trusting the process and the timing of what's happening in your life. Your empowered feminine energy is your intuition, your sensitivity, and your healthy vulnerability. Empowered feminine energy is about going inward. It's nurturing, self-reflective, relationship oriented, process and journey oriented, versus goal oriented. It's about being in the flow.

***Your empowered feminine energy is about being present in your body, and staying connected to your feelings. It's being emotionally present to yourself and to others.*** It's creative, understanding, nonjudgmental, and unconditionally loving both to yourself and others. It's also being able to surrender, not surrender as in giving up, but surrender as in *letting go.* More on this with secret seven. It's being in your heart and having an open heart. It's having empathy. It's a leaning back kind of energy, meaning you're not trying to force or make something to happen. Yet it's not about doing nothing, because ***it's about getting really in touch with your body and all of your senses, your feelings, your heart, your intuition, your emotional needs and your healthy vulnerability—and that's a lot!***

When you are in your empowered feminine energy, you listen to and trust your intuition and respond to it. You express how you're feeling and what you need and want without making someone else wrong, without criticizing, judging, or blaming. When you're in your empowered feminine energy you have a very loving relationship with yourself. You believe that you can have what you want in relationships and in life and that you are worthy of having what you want. *These are all powerful aspects of your empowered feminine energy.*

## Empowered Masculine Energy

*An empowered woman also has her own empowered masculine energy that supports her empowered feminine energy.* Empowered masculine energy, is a doing energy, rather than a state of simply being. You're taking action; you follow the steps you need to take; you follow through. It's also goal, achievement, and accomplishment oriented, instead of journey and process oriented. It is the opposite of the feeling and emotional energy of your feminine energy. Instead, masculine energy is about thinking; it's mental energy. When you're in your masculine energy, you're logical, analytical, and rational. You're planning, scheduling, and making decisions. Empowered masculine energy is naturally competitive in a healthy way, meaning you want to succeed and win. It is advising, managing, or supervising. When you're giving and serving others without an agenda, that's empowered masculine energy. It's the energy of initiating, leadership, and service. It's more of a leaning forward energy, rather than the leaning back of empowered feminine energy.

When someone is in their empowered masculine energy, their words are backed up by and match their actions. They keep their commitments; they have clarity; they set healthy boundaries. They're assertive. They provide structure and stability. Empowered masculine energy has a deep desire to fulfill the desires of the feminine and to increase her happiness. Empowered masculine energy is also a providing energy, in other words, someone in their empowered masculine energy loves to *provide* for their loved ones in many ways, financially and otherwise. It's taking good care of loved ones and it has a very protective energy. *You can say that empowered masculine energy is protective, proactive and productive. And lastly, empowered masculine energy respects, cherishes, appreciates, and values women and feminine energy.*

If you're attracted to and want to attract men or people with empowered masculine energy, then you'll want to be connected to your empowered feminine energy because opposite energies attract. You also need to support your empowered feminine energy with your own empowered masculine energy because *the relationship between these two energies within yourself will often be reflected in your outer relationships.* For example, if you tend to be critical of yourself—disempowered masculine energy—you will often attract the same in a partner, i.e., someone who is critical of you. And if you're needy, codependent, and lacking in self-love—disempowered feminine energy—then you're more likely to attract men and people with disempowered masculine energy who may be self-absorbed, controlling, and emotionally unavailable.

*Ultimately, you want to find the blend of empowered masculine and empowered feminine energies within you and in your relationships that feels natural and good to you.*

I'll be inviting you to become aware of your energy in *many different ways* throughout this book. Noticing when you're in disempowered masculine or feminine energy, so you can bring yourself back into your empowered energies, is just one of the ways. Awareness is always the first step to changing anything.

*Don't worry if the concepts of masculine and feminine energy or working with the energy in your seven chakras seems a bit abstract to you now. As you read through the book and begin awakening your power in each chakra, how to practically apply what you learn and how to make the changes you want in your energy, relationships and life will become very clear and easy to understand.*

## KEY PRINCIPLE NUMBER FIVE – LOVE IS YOUR POWER

*Becoming an empowered woman and making the changes you want starts with your connection to yourself. Connecting with yourself is loving yourself, and loving yourself is healing yourself.* Love is ultimately the energy that will empower and transform every part of you—your body, your relationships and your life. Being an empowered woman is not about becoming something you're not. It is not about needing to "fix" yourself. You're already powerful, whether you're aware of it right now or not. On an energetic and cellular level, you are literally made from the energy of love. You just need to remove the blockages to the love and power inside yourself and remember your true nature and who you really are!

Your relationship with yourself (self-love) and your relationship with your Spiritual Source (Divine Love) are your greatest powers. This love is ever present. Both self-love and Divine Love are always available to you through your connection to your own heart. You always have the choice to choose love or to come back to love when you slip away and shift into fear. *Self-love involves loving, accepting, and staying connected to all parts of you—your body, your feelings, your needs, your intuition, and your heart's desires, as you will be learning throughout the rest of this book.*

# SEVEN SECRETS OF THE EMPOWERED WOMAN

The next seven chapters will correspond to each of your seven chakras and will teach you the seven secrets to becoming a more empowered woman. All seven secrets are interconnected, and each secret builds upon the prior chapter's secret. Please read the chapters in order the first time. After your first reading of the entire book, you can go back and reread the specific chapter that you need. For example, if you are feeling some anxiety or fear, refer to chapter one or seven again. If you find yourself emotionally reacting, reread chapter two.

*Within each chapter you will find empowered woman practices to help you apply some of what you have learned.* At the end of each chapter there is a brief summary about how being in your power in that particular chakra helps you to create the healthy love and healthy life you want and deserve. There is also a list of empowered woman mantras to help you reprogram your subconscious mind and change your energy with love.

**Secret One** is about the power of grounding, feeling safe and secure within yourself, and being able to trust yourself, life, and others. It's also about the power of loving and trusting your body.

**Secret Two** is about awakening and embracing your empowered feminine energy and the power of mastering your emotions.

**Secret Three** is about increasing your self-confidence and self-esteem, changing false beliefs, and the power of having healthy boundaries and standards.

**Secret Four** is about accepting your lovability and the power of your heart and love: self-love, relationship love, and Divine Love.

**Secret Five** is about empowered loving communication, embracing your healthy vulnerability, and learning how to speak your truth with love.

**Secret Six** is about manifesting what your heart desires with your intuition, imagination and empowered feminine energy.

**Secret Seven** is about releasing fear-based attachments, co-creating your life with a Higher Power (or whatever name you call the Divine), and having faith.

**To reinforce everything you read and learn, please be sure to download the *Empowered Woman Within* guided meditation - a free companion to this book.** It is a 35-minute guided journey through your chakras first to clear energy blockages and then to program your subconscious mind with new, healing and empowering feelings, beliefs and behavior patterns. It includes beautiful background music with sound healing binaural beats to facilitate deep receptivity to the spoken words. Listen with headphones seated or lying down for deep relaxation and body-mind-spirit healing or play in the background for healing and inspiration while you walk, exercise or practice yoga. It's excellent to listen to before sleep, before a date, before an important meeting or event, or whenever you want to increase your self-confidence, as well as your inner glow, radiance and attractiveness. Information about how to receive your free guided meditation is at the end of the book.

Are you ready to learn about the seven secrets to becoming a more empowered woman? To truly love yourself and manifest the healthy love and life you want and deserve, from the inside out? I'm guessing that since this book somehow found its way into your hands, your answer is a definite YES. ***Let's get started!***

# EMPOWERED WOMAN
## SECRET ONE

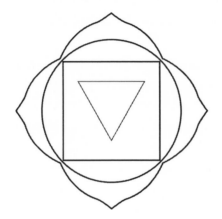

# CHAKRA ONE

*Grounding, Loving Your Body, Cultivating a Sense of Safety, Security, and Trust Within Yourself*

# CHAPTER ONE
# SECRET ONE

Your journey starts with chakra one, secret one. The first empowered woman secret to creating the healthy love and life you want and deserve corresponds with your first energy center and is called your *root chakra*. It's located energetically at the base of your spine, and the color associated with it is ruby red. This energy center is about trust, safety and security, your basic survival needs, your physical body and physical health and feeling a sense of belonging, support and prosperity. This is the home of your subconscious programming from your first seven years of life.

## CHAKRA ONE - IN YOUR POWER

***When you are in your power in this center, you feel a basic sense of safety and security within yourself.*** It's not that you never feel fear; you do, but most of the time it doesn't completely overpower or overwhelm you. You are grounded and centered. You are present in your body in this moment, rather than being in your head worrying about the future or thinking about the past.

You feel a basic sense of trust in life, and you trust that your needs will be met. You trust yourself, and you also have the ability to trust others appropriately, without having blind trust or being afraid to trust anyone. You feel supported by others and the Universe and you have a sense of belonging in the world. You have a prosperity consciousness when it comes to money and other forms of support. Being in your power in this center means that you love, trust and take good care of your body and your health. In other words, you have a very loving relationship with your body.

## CHAKRA ONE - NOT IN YOUR POWER

You are not in your power in this first center when you are ungrounded, completely over-whelmed by fear, and when your fears have a lot of power over you. You often feel a lack of safety and make decisions from a place of fear and insecurity. You lack trust in yourself and may have difficulty trusting others. When you are not in your power in this first center, you are disconnected from and critical of your body, and you may not take very good care of your health. You may have a "lack" consciousness, feeling that there's never enough money or time. You can feel unsupported or that you don't belong and are all alone in this world. You may be in a chronic state of stress or fear, which can cause you to become physically exhausted or contribute to health challenges.

*The first secret to becoming a more empowered woman and to creating the healthy love and life you want and deserve is about getting or staying grounded, cultivating trust, releasing the fear or anxiety that you have from your past or about whatever is going on in your life right now and learning how to cultivate a basic sense of safety and security within yourself.*

## GROUNDING

It's very hard to trust, release fear, or feel safe if you're not grounded and present in your body, so let's start with grounding.

**What is grounding?** Grounding is connecting with the energy of the earth, connecting with your physical body and becoming more present in this moment, right here and right now, whatever you are doing. Grounding is becoming aware of the downward flow of energy moving through your body, from the top of your head, all the way down through your legs, feet and into the earth. The earth is always here supporting you simply through the force of gravity. Grounding is the experience of being at home in your body, especially in the lower half of your body. When you're fully present in your body and present in this moment, your nervous system will relax, which leads me to the second question.

**Why is it important for you to be grounded?** If you're not grounded and present in your body, you will start to feel very anxious, just as a toddler gets anxious when she thinks her mother is gone. Grounding helps you to relax and to release tension and stress. Part of the reason for this is because "mother" earth has a very slow, nurturing vibration, so connecting with it helps you to relax. Grounding and present moment awareness will help you tune in and connect with yourself on all levels. It helps you become more aware of your body and your emotions, brings you a sense of peace and calm, settles your nervous system, calms your mind, and helps you feel more safe, stable, and secure within yourself.

**It's especially important to be grounded, present, and connected to yourself when you are interacting with other people.** This way you can observe people and partners or potential partners while noticing how you are feeling. Grounding helps you to stay in touch with your intuition, be aware of your own body and feelings, and more carefully evaluate the people and environment around you.

When you're not grounded, you're like a tree without roots. You can be easily triggered off your center and out of your power into a state of confusion, stress, fear or anxiety, and emotional reactivity. You will feel unsafe and unprotected. You will feel more powerless rather than powerful. When you are ungrounded, you will lack strong boundaries and can more easily absorb or be affected by the energy of other people. Grounding actually protects your energy and prevents you from absorbing negative energy or stress from other people or the environment around you.

Overall, the less grounded you are, the more anxiety, stress, worry, lack of focus, and obsessive thinking you will experience. Your breathing will be shallow. The more grounded you are, the calmer you will feel in your body and in your mind. You will have more mental clarity, more resilience, and be more connected to your intuitive guidance.

**Grounding also helps you heal your physical body because it helps you to feel a sense of safety, trust, and peace and it's very nurturing for your body.** This fosters your overall health and is very good for your adrenals, your nervous system, and your hormones. If you have a lot of trouble grounding or you feel ungrounded and anxious often, it usually means that some healing needs to be done, that you're experiencing a lot of stress, or that you're in a big life transition, such as when you move or lose your job. When you're experiencing a big change, it will be more challenging for you to ground. If that is the case, you will need to focus on consciously grounding yourself even more. So how do you ground yourself? Experiment with the following practices.

## EMPOWERED WOMAN GROUNDING PRACTICES AND SUGGESTIONS

**1. The very first thing to do to ground yourself and to stay grounded is to slow down as you go about your day, no matter what you are doing, and to become very present in this moment.** If you slow down enough, it will help you to remember and feel that there is a supportive energy available to you at all times through your connection to the earth. Pay attention to whatever it is that you're doing and be aware of what you're feeling, seeing, hearing, etc.

**2. As you go through the day remind yourself to feel and be more present in your body, especially the lower half of your body, by consciously bringing some of your attention into your hips, your low belly, your legs and your feet.** Feel your feet on the ground and breathe deep and slow. Breathing is very helpful for grounding because when you bring your attention to your breath, it automatically brings your attention into your body and into the present moment. As you breathe, sense or imagine the downward flow of energy that starts at the top of your head and flows down through your whole body, into your legs, out the bottoms of your feet, and into the earth. Feeling or imagining this downward flow of energy will help you ground because your energy follows your intention, or in other words, where your attention goes your energy flows.

**3. Make grounding the first part of any kind of prayer or meditation practice that you do.** Using the imagery described above, imagine, feel and direct a downward flow of energy in your body from the top of your head, through your whole body and out through your feet into the earth. Alternatively, when you are seated you can imagine a tree trunk around your hips and the base of your spine that flows all the way down into the earth. You may want to imagine a beautiful beam of light starting at the base of your spine that wraps around your hips, low back, and abdominal area and then see or feel it flowing deep down into the center of the earth. Your body's energy will respond to what you imagine.

The energy of the earth is always there, but because we live in a chaotic, stressful world, it's easy to get ungrounded and disconnected from yourself and from the earth's energy. Again, grounding is about being really present in your body, right here and right now in this moment. It is an ongoing practice. As you practice grounding, you will notice how calming it is and how it helps you to feel more relaxed.

**4. Remember, if you are always thinking about the future and the past, not only are you missing what is actually happening in the present moment, but you are also missing that slow, calming, supportive and stable energy of the earth.** Remember to consciously bring your awareness into your body rather than always being up in your head thinking. Remind yourself that thinking is masculine energy, and you want to some spend time in your empowered feminine energy which includes connecting with your body, your feelings, and the supportive, nurturing, energy of Mother Earth.

**5. Another great way to ground is to spend some time in nature.** Spending time in nature can definitely help you ground and connect with the slow calming vibration of the earth. You can also release fear, tension or stress by imagining or affirming that when you exhale you are breathing any fear or stress down through your grounding cord, out of your body, and into the earth. You can do this when out in nature or as part of your prayer or meditation practice at home. Remember your energy flows where your attention goes. The earth will transform the energy that you release.

## LOVE, SAFETY AND BELONGING

*Your first chakra is the home of your subconscious core beliefs and emotions related to love, safety and belonging.* It holds programming from your first seven years of life, particularly how you bonded, connected to, and related with your parents or primary caregivers and what you learned from those relationships.

*We all need love, safety and a sense of belonging and have developed beliefs about them.* Your parents were like God to you in the first seven years of your life because you needed them to keep you alive. Let's say, for example, that you felt like you had to walk around on eggshells when you were little to keep your dad from getting angry. If this was the case, you might have developed the belief that you need to be a perfect little girl in order to be safe and loved.

As a little girl you internalized everything, meaning that whatever happened to you and around you, you took it personally and thought it had to do with you. If your dad was emotionally unavailable when you were a child, you probably felt that was because you weren't worthy of his emotional support and presence. If something happened or someone did something to you that was not okay, you as a child translated that to, "I'm not okay," and you will feel a sense of shame or unworthiness on a subconscious level. And if you feel like you're not okay or good enough or that you're not safe, you won't be very present in your body. You won't be very grounded.

*The good news is that now as an adult woman you can ground yourself and become more present in your body, cultivating a sense of safety and security within yourself.* This will also help you become more aware of what some of the false, subconscious beliefs are that you accepted or formed at a very young age such as the belief, "If I want to be safe and loved, I have to please everyone." That's a false belief, and once you become aware of your beliefs you can decide whether or not they are serving you. If not, you can change and reprogram them. You will be learning how to do this with secret three in chapter three. As I mentioned in the introduction, all seven secrets and chakras are interconnected!

## RELEASING FEAR WITH THE POWER OF LOVE

*It is normal for human beings to feel some fear.* In addition to old, subconscious programming related to love, safety and belonging from your first seven years of life, you may also have fear, anxiety or worries about whatever is currently happening or not happening in your life right now. We will go a little deeper with understanding and transforming fear and other emotions in the next chapter. For now, when you find yourself feeling fear, worry or anxiety about whatever is going on in your life (not an actual dangerous or threatening situation), remember how powerful and supported you are. It's easy to forget this and how many options you have.

*Here are two empowering questions that you can ask yourself to prevent your fears from overwhelming you and help shift your energy with love.* When fear arises connect with the love and power that you have within you. How? First get grounded and keep your awareness in the present moment. Place your hand on your heart and connect with it as you take some deep breaths. *Next, ask yourself, what part of this situation can you control? In other words, what are the options you have and what actions can you take?*

When you take positive action, the Universe steps up to meet you. If you're worried and fearful about not being able to find the work and money that you need (definitely a first chakra issue), take action steps such as sending out resumes. Renewing old connections and letting people know you are looking for work is another positive step.

You also have some control over your mindset and your attitude. For example, you can perceive the loss of your job as the worst thing that ever happened to you or as an opportunity for you to find work that is even more enjoyable and meaningful. Release the part of your challenges that you cannot control to your Spiritual Source, and trust that you will be guided and supported through whatever you are facing. Focusing on what you can control moves you back into a position of power instead of being overcome by your own fears.

*The second question to ask yourself is what kind of support do you have in your life right now?* Bring to mind all of the supportive people in your life—friends, family, a teacher, counselor or coach, etc. Connect with your Spiritual Source for support, comfort and guidance through some form of prayer or meditation, or by going somewhere that helps you to feel the loving, supportive energy of the earth, such as being out in nature or near the ocean. While focusing on your heart, feel gratitude and appreciation for this support. Gratitude has been shown to reduce fear and anxiety. If you feel that you don't have enough support, reach out for help from others. It is a sign of strength not weakness to seek out the kind of support you need, and when you ask you shall receive.

Doing all of the above—grounding, deep breathing, keeping your attention in the present moment, taking action toward what you can control, feeling grateful for the support you have or reaching out for the support you need, and releasing what you cannot control to your Spiritual Source, will help you to feel more empowered. You will start to realize that you are more powerful than your fears and that you can choose where you put your attention. Focus your attention on love. Love is more powerful than fear. Know and trust that your soul came here to this earth with all of the inner resources you need to be able to handle anything that you experience here. Remember that you are meant both to be supported by others in your outer world as well as to receive support and guidance from your Spiritual Source. *You are stronger and more capable than you may think or feel at times. There is a very wise, strong and powerful woman inside of you!*

## MONEY FEARS

If your fears are specifically related to money, there are many books and programs out there to help you develop a prosperity consciousness. It is not necessary for you to have or be making a lot of money to be in your power in this first chakra. What you need is to have an *abundance consciousness,* a trust that your needs will be met and gratitude for what you do have, rather than having a "lack" consciousness and focusing on what you don't have.

## HEALTH-RELATED FEARS AND IMPORTANT DECISIONS

Being an empowered woman in chakra one includes taking good care of your physical body and your health. This involves eating a healthy diet and exercising, in addition to all of the important secrets you are learning about in this book. If your fears are health related, I suggest learning more about the power of your mind to help you heal or prevent disease and about the power of the body-mind connection. There are many good books and programs on these topics also.

Keep in mind that whenever you have an important decision to make, whether it's about your health or anything else, you do not want to make that decision from the energy of fear. If you do so, you will often regret your decision. Make sure you get grounded, calm and centered so you can tune in to your intuition and make your decision from the energy of love. This can be easier said than done, but everything you learn in this book will help you to do this. You will be learning about your intuition in chapter six.

## TRUSTING YOURSELF, OTHERS AND YOUR SPIRITUAL SOURCE

*Choosing to trust will help you release all kinds of fear.* It will help you feel safe and to be in your power as a woman in this first chakra. Trust is an energy that lives in your heart. When you feel anxious and have fearful thoughts running through your head, bring your attention down into your heart. When you are empowered, you can choose to trust that somehow everything is going to be okay and that all of your needs will be met. Trust your Spiritual Source, trust yourself, and you will have the ability to trust others. Let's discuss these three interconnected aspects of trust.

## TRUSTING LIFE AND YOUR SPIRITUAL SOURCE

Do you trust that there is Loving Presence, a Spiritual Source, whatever name you call it, that is always with you, supporting and guiding you? Do you trust that your challenges are

opportunities for emotional and spiritual growth? Can you trust that no matter how difficult things seem, that all is in Divine Perfect Order?

***Trust is a peaceful, internal state that you can connect with inside your own heart.*** You can
tap into the energy of trust when you are grounded and practice present moment awareness
and when you connect with your heart and your Spiritual Source. It is a conscious choice to
cultivate this connection. It's like tuning in to a specific radio station. Trust can help you to
release fear and anxiety. You are always surrounded by a Divine Loving Energy. This Loving
Energy is both within you and around you at the same time. You just need to become aware
of it, call upon it, and tune in to it. One of the best ways to do this is with prayer or meditation. More on this with secret seven in chapter seven.

***Again, you have a calm, peaceful center within you, and that center resides in your own
heart.*** There is research by the Heart Math Institute that shows when you bring your awareness into your heart, it brings your brain and your nervous system into a calm, relaxed, and
balanced state. You then vibrate at a higher frequency. Research has also shown that when
you place one or two hands on your heart, your body releases a relaxing hormone called
oxytocin, the same hormone that is produced when you are pleasantly touched or hugged
by others.

When you are in this calm, heart-centered state, you will start to feel more peaceful and
your anxiety will lessen. It takes practice, especially when you are experiencing life challenges and feeling fear or stress, but the more you connect with your heart and trust, the
more receptive you become, and remember receptivity is empowered feminine energy. The
more you allow your life to unfold—allowing is also empowered feminine energy—rather
than resisting and trying to control everything, the more at peace you will feel. This will
also bring about a greater sense of safety and security within yourself and make you more
attractive and magnetic. ***Trusting is empowered feminine energy!***

If you are resisting life and trying to control everything, you are not trusting. If this is an
issue for you, try the following empowered woman practice.

## EMPOWERED WOMAN PRACTICE FOR CULTIVATING TRUST

Place one or both hands on your heart as you bring your attention down from your head and into your heart. Next, ask yourself, "How would I feel right now if I chose to trust that I am going to be okay, that things will work out for me, even if right now I don't know when or how?" When you connect with your heart, you realize that nothing else really exists but the present moment and that there is always an energy of trust inside your heart that you can tap into. You can consciously choose to trust that everything is unfolding perfectly and working out for your highest good. Choosing to trust is an ongoing spiritual practice, just as is choosing love instead of fear.

## LEARNING TO TRUST YOURSELF

*The more grounded you are, the safer and more secure you will feel within, and the more you connect with your heart and your Spiritual Source, the more you will be able to trust yourself.* Do you trust yourself in one aspect of your life but not in another part of your life? Perhaps you trust your decisions at work, but because you experienced a painful relationship in the past, you aren't able to trust yourself in relationships. What you want to do in this case is ask yourself what you learned in that past relationship. The way that we stop repeating painful patterns is to learn and grow from our experiences.

Look at everything that happens to you as a learning experience. You don't have to be perfect to trust yourself. As you learn and grow, you will stop repeating painful patterns. *The more time you spend tuning in to your body, feelings, and intuition—being in your empowered feminine energy—the more you will strengthen your trust in yourself.*

When you are trying to decide what to do in any situation, place one or both hands on your heart. This will help you tune in to what is going on inside of you rather than remaining in your head and trying to figure out what you "should" do. Anytime you hear yourself saying "I should," you are in your head, not in your heart, and you are not connected to your feelings. When you are grounded, present in, and connected to your body and your feelings, you will notice when something doesn't feel right or good to you sooner than if you tried to think your way through it.

*Ask yourself often throughout your day, "How do I really feel about this?"* Tune in to your body—how does it feel? Ask yourself, "How do I really feel about this person or this situation? How does this decision really feel in my heart and in my soul? What do I need to know or do here?" As you ask for and receive answers to these questions you'll begin to trust yourself and all of the wisdom that you have within you. Even if you don't know what to do next in a particular situation, trust that the guidance you need will come to you when the time is right. You will learn more about the power of your intuition with secret six in chapter six.

## TRUSTING YOURSELF - THE PREREQUISITE FOR TRUSTING OTHERS

A common question my coaching clients or students have asked me is, "How do I trust others, especially men, if I've been hurt?" The answer is that you must focus on first learning to trust yourself. When you trust yourself, you know that no matter what happens with someone else, you will be able to handle it and learn from it.

*Trusting yourself involves learning how to listen to and trust your intuition. Many women talk themselves out of trusting their intuition and then regret it later.* Getting more in touch with your empowered feminine energy will help you trust both yourself and to appropriately trust others. The goal is really to trust yourself, not the other person. Each situation in which you honor your intuition will be a learning experience that will help you develop more trust in yourself over time.

So please allow yourself to make mistakes rather than trying to trust everyone or to be constantly looking for certainty. If you do that, you will suffer because life is by nature uncertain. If you're always looking for certainty outside yourself, you will be setting yourself up for frustration most of the time, and you'll likely fall into a controlling kind of energy which comes from fear. Not only does this not feel good, it's also not a very attractive or confident energy when you're wanting to attract a partner or other opportunities to you.

Developing trust in yourself and in your own intuition is the key because it frees you up from having to know everything that is going to happen and when it's going to happen. Instead, you allow things to unfold naturally and to let people to be who they are. As you observe others, you trust that you will know how to respond in an authentic, powerful and loving way. *You can't control what other people do—they have free will—so learning to trust yourself and your intuition is the key and a life skill well worth developing.*

## YOUR HISTORY IS NOT YOUR DESTINY

Another part of trusting yourself is knowing that any unfulfilling or painful experience or relationship you have had does not determine your future. Sometimes we fear that bad experiences from the past will happen again, but that is not the case if you are learning from your mistakes and growing. This is a part of your feminine wisdom and power. *Know that any challenge or difficult experience you have had or are having now is happening to help empower you, to show you what you need to learn or what you need to change to be able to fulfill your heart's desires.*

The more you tune in to your body and your feelings, the more you will be able to trust yourself to know when something feels good and when something does not feel good to you. You will trust yourself to set boundaries and to remove yourself from situations and relationships that don't feel good to you. More on healthy boundaries with secret three in chapter three.

*Your history is not your destiny, so please don't close down your heart if you've been hurt.* To do so is to cut yourself off from your own empowered feminine wisdom, which you have access to through your heart. You always have the opportunity to turn any pain you have been through into power. Life is a journey and the more you trust yourself, your connection to your Divine Source and the guidance you receive from your own heart and soul, the more you will know who you can trust in a relationship.

Protecting yourself and being distrustful are not the answers to having a healthy relationship or a joyful life. When you are fearful and distrusting of others, you are not actually protecting yourself, especially if you close off your heart which is the center of your intuitive intelligence. On the other hand, blind trust in others is not the answer either because it can put you more at risk for being hurt. When you open your heart there's always a risk of being hurt, but you can reduce that risk greatly the more you become aware of and change your disempowering relationship patterns.

## REPROGRAMMING FALSE BELIEFS HELPS YOU TO TRUST

So, how can you trust others appropriately without shutting down and building walls up around your heart? The answer is usually to reparent your inner child or reprogram the false beliefs and repetitive emotions that have caused you to live in a state of fear too often. For example, if deep down you fear that you can't survive alone or you haven't learned how to find a sense of safety and security within yourself, then you may get involved too quickly and over invest in a relationship. You can then miss the early warning signs of untrustworthiness because of your old fears and survival programs from the first seven years of your life—beliefs of which you may not even be consciously aware. This is why it's so important to become aware your early programming and to do the inner healing work. More on how to do this in upcoming chapters.

The fear that you can't survive alone or that you're not safe is most likely coming from the little girl inside you. This can cause you to subconsciously look for a partner to be like a parent. Releasing your old hurts and fears will help you to become a more empowered woman and to know who you can trust. As an empowered adult woman, if a man is not giving you the kind of love you want in a relationship, you can walk away and create a healthy loving relationship with someone else. It's important to understand that sometimes people are just *not capable* of giving you what you want and deserve.

When you connect with your *Empowered Woman Within*, you have a basic sense of happiness, love, safety and security within yourself, then a partner can *add* to that and you will feel even happier, more loved, even safer, and more secure. You want to keep tuning in to your needs, feelings, and desires, trusting your body and your intuition, and committing to healing and loving yourself. You want to show up in your power, which is with love, starting with *self-love*. This includes being honest with people about your feelings or concerns, asking difficult questions, setting healthy boundaries, and communicating what you need or desire.

*You do not want to be desperate, needy, or codependent, which is disempowered feminine energy. At the same time, you do not want to be controlling, because that is disempowered masculine energy.* If you are in either of these fear-based disempowered energies, you will often over invest in or over commit to a man or person too soon. *Trust builds over time in a relationship, and you want to maintain your life, your boundaries, and move at a reasonable, pace, taking things slowly.* If a man doesn't want to slow down or respect your healthy boundaries, then he is either needy or codependent himself or he's very self-absorbed, and you definitely don't want to have a relationship with such a person!

The bottom line is as you release your fears you won't be giving your power away to a man by making him your ultimate source of love, safety, and happiness. You will be able to choose healthy loving relationships and walk away from them if they are not very healthy or enjoyable. You will slowly emotionally invest yourself in a man or a friendship, knowing that at any time you can and will walk away if it's not good for you. When you have your own back and know that you will protect yourself with healthy boundaries (your empowered masculine energy) then you will be able to open your heart and begin to trust others (empowered feminine energy). In other words when your own empowered masculine energy is supporting your empowered feminine energy, you will be able to trust and open your heart to love.

*Instead of living in fear, wondering if someone is trustworthy, or if they are going to hurt you, focus on taking care of yourself, making sure you don't over commit or over invest too soon.* Take the time to observe people or potential partners. Does a man keep his word—does he do what he says he is going to do? If he does, that's one sign of trustworthiness. As an empowered woman you know that a man is always doing the best he can given his own wounds and that it is not your responsibility to fix or heal him. Instead, become aware of what is going on within you and what your relationship with him is bringing up for you to acknowledge, change or heal. *Your responsibility is to learn how to love and trust yourself, which brings us to the next topic because this includes loving and trusting your physical body.*

## LOVING AND TRUSTING YOUR BODY

In addition to grounding, trust, safety and support, your first chakra is about your physical body and your physical health. Most women have great difficulty loving their bodies uncon- ditionally just as they are. I really can't emphasize enough how important it is to *practice loving your body. This is a choice and a commitment.* Your body is the amazing vessel of your spirit, and you have the body that you were meant to have in this lifetime. Stop criticizing your body! Remember criticism is your disempowered masculine energy and that will often cause you to attract men with disempowered masculine energy who are critical of you, mirroring back to you your relationship with yourself. *Accepting your perceived physical imperfections is a big part of being an empowered woman.*

Make no mistake about it, your body knows the thoughts you have about it, and it feels the feelings you have about it. The cells in your body respond to your words, thoughts and feel- ings. Start to notice what you say about your body, whether in your head or out loud. Your body is alive and conscious. If you're criticizing your body, it will not feel safe, and therefore it won't be able to relax, heal, or release fear. *Would you feel safe and relaxed around someone who criticizes you or your body?* When you criticize your body, you are automatically disconnecting from it. This blocks your ability to be in tune with your intuition and the guidance that your body is giving you all the time when you are tuned in enough to hear, sense, or feel it.

## EMPOWERED WOMAN PRACTICE FOR LOVING YOUR BODY

Whenever you catch yourself saying or thinking something critical about your body, first apologize out loud to it and then say something loving and kind to your body instead. I call this body-love talk. Everyday commit to this practice. *It's really a choice to love your body.*

If you find yourself saying or feeling that you don't like your legs for example, start by choosing to feel grateful that you have legs. Apologize to them, telling them that you are so sorry you criticized them. Next begin sending your legs love and thanking your legs for all that they do for you. This is an ongoing practice. Most women think that they cannot love their body until—until they lose weight, until it is heathier, etc. But you will have a very hard time make lasting changes with your body unless you are making those changes *with the energy of love,* and criticism is not love. Changes made with the energy of criticism rarely if ever last. *Changes that are loved into being are more permanent.*

In addition to apologizing when you catch yourself criticizing your body, try this: Close your eyes and place one or both hands on your heart. This will connect you to the energy of love and compassion. *It will be hard to keep criticizing yourself with one or both hands on your heart.* Connect with the love inside your heart so you can learn how to embody self-love. You can literally choose to bring self-love into your body and into your life at any time for healing and transformation.

## SELF-LOVE IS ALWAYS AVAILABLE TO YOU

*It is something that you can tap into and generate anytime.* Your body, exactly as it is right now, is innately worthy of love. You want to love and cherish it no matter your age, the shape your body is in, how much you weigh, your size etc. One of the reasons it's so difficult for many women to love their body is because the media is always sending us messages that only a specific body shape, age, and size is acceptable and attractive. Do not buy into this and compare yourself to false images of perfection!

*You can experience deep self-love in every cell of your body whenever you choose, but it is a choice that you must make every single moment of every single day.* The bottom line is, do you want to continue living in a body that you judge and criticize, constantly feeling like you're not good enough, not accepting yourself, and remaining in a state of fear? Or do you want to live in your body with love while creating better health, beauty, and vitality from unconditional love? The choice is always yours.

*The more you love your body, the healthier you become and the more confident and attractive you become.* You have the power to send love to your whole body or to a specific part of your body, and when you do, it will create a sense of safety. Your body will relax, your hormonal system will balance, and your immune system will get stronger. It's how you feel about your body that is attractive, not what you weigh or what size dress you wear, etc. It's how you feel and what you're thinking about your body that makes you attractive. Remember everything is energy and people feel your energy.

When you send your body love on a regular basis, you're going to naturally want to eat healthier or exercise more. You will then start to feel better and better. It will become a wonderful cycle because you'll be creating changes in your body with the energy of self-love instead of self-criticism. Please write the following sentence down and read it as often as needed. *To have a body that I love, I begin by loving the body that I have.*

## EMPOWERED WOMAN BODY WISDOM PRACTICE

Having a loving relationship and connection with your body will improve your health and your relationships. You have answers and empowered feminine wisdom within you and within your body. Practice asking your body a question and notice what the immediate response is in your body. As you learn to tune in to your body, it will tell you what foods you need to eat, the people you need to be around or not be around. Notice whether your body tenses up, contracts, or feels heavy when you ask it a question. If so, that is your body's way of saying no; this is not good for you. But if you ask your body about something and you instead get a feeling of expansion, strength, ease, or peace, then you know your body is saying yes, this is good.

Take very good care of your body and your health. As a woman, you are highly intuitive, and your body is highly intuitive: that's how wise and intelligent it is. It is an amazing beautiful instrument and the temple of your soul. Trust in its phenomenal ability to heal itself and to protect you from disease. Speak to your body with kindness, gratitude and love. Ask it questions and tune in to its responses, then trust the guidance it gives you and the wisdom it holds. ***Know that your body doesn't lie.***

### SECRET ONE SUMMARY

**How Being in Your Power in Chakra One Helps You Create the Healthy Love and Life You Want and Deserve**

**Health:** Grounding, trusting, releasing fear, and feeling safe relaxes your body and calms your nervous system. It helps strengthen your immune system and adrenal glands and helps you cope better with stress, all of which improves your health. Loving your body relaxes and heals your body. Tuning into and listening to your body gives you intuitive guidance that can help you make important decisions about your health. Loving your body will also help you reduce physical pain or lose weight, if desired.

**Love and Relationships**: Being grounded and centered and trusting yourself helps you to stay present first to yourself and then to others. It is the foundation for your empowered woman self. It helps you respond instead of react. It helps you to tune in and listen to your intuition and become aware of any red flags when dating or in other situations. It helps you to take things slowly in a relationship and allow trust to build over time. It helps you to stay in the moment and not over commit or over invest your energy in a relationship too soon. Loving your body, whatever your age, shape or size, makes you more attractive to others. When you feel a sense of safety and security within yourself, you will not stay in a relationship too long or give your power away by making someone else your ultimate source of safety and security.

## CHAKRA ONE EMPOWERED WOMAN MANTRAS

*I am grounded.*
*I am safe.*
*I am supported.*
*I feel safe and secure.*
*I am present in this moment and in my body.*
*I am healthy and strong.*
*I have an abundance consciousness.*
*I love my body.*
*I trust my body.*
*I sleep well.*
*I trust life.*
*I trust myself.*
*I love my life.*
*I always have all that I need.*
*I feel a deep sense of safety and security within me.*

You have learned a lot in this chapter. You have learned how to ground yourself, how to cultivate a sense of safety and security within yourself, how to trust yourself, how to trust life, how to trust others appropriately and how to practice loving and trusting your body. You are now ready to move on to secret two, chakra two, which includes learning more specifically about how to awaken and embrace your empowered feminine energy and also learning how to master your emotions.

# EMPOWERED WOMAN
# **SECRET TWO**

# CHAKRA TWO

*Awakening and Embracing Your Empowered Feminine*
*Energy and Mastering Your Emotions*

# CHAPTER TWO
# SECRET TWO

Welcome to secret number two, chakra two. The second empowered woman secret to creating the healthy love and life you want and deserve corresponds with your second chakra. This is often called your feminine power center, because it is the chakra that governs and is the home of your feminine energy. You have feminine energy throughout your whole body, but this is where it comes from and where it is stored. This chakra is located in the center of your pelvis and the color is a beautiful bright orange. This power center is about your feelings and emotions, your needs and vulnerability. These are all aspects of your empowered feminine energy.

**This chakra is what allows you to feel what's happening emotionally in yourself and in others**. It also includes your sensuality and sexuality. Sensuality is not the same thing as sexuality. The sensual part of you is the part that experiences something as being pleasing or fulfilling to all your senses, not just your sense of touch. It could be appreciating the beautiful aroma of a rose, the sight of a gorgeous sunset, or the sound of some beautiful music, as well as enjoying the loving, tender touch of your partner.

**This chakra is also about your passion and your creativity.** The energy of this center is very powerful because you literally have the ability to create a new life inside this area of your body!

## CHAKRA TWO - IN YOUR POWER

*When you are in your power in this center you are emotionally present to yourself and then to others*. You allow yourself to feel your emotions, instead of making them wrong, repressing them, emotionally abandoning yourself, judging yourself, or projecting them onto other people. *This doesn't mean that you necessarily express them to a person at the time or that you take any action.* You have a loving relationship with your emotions, just as you have a loving relationship with your body. You know how to work with your painful emotional states when you get triggered and you have the ability to shift them and come back to your center, back into emotional balance. ***Your emotions do not control you, instead you are the master of your emotions, meaning you are able to respond with love rather than react with fear most of the time.***

You do not dwell on, stay stuck in or drown in your painful emotions. You transform them as quickly as possible and learn from them. You know that you have the power to choose how you want to feel. You are aware of the hurts or unmet needs of the little girl inside of you and you are learning how to reparent and be a loving mother to this part of yourself. This helps you to make decisions and respond to others from your empowered woman self. You have emotional and sexual boundaries. You don't take on or absorb the emotional energy of others. You embrace both your sensuality and sexuality. You embrace your empowered feminine energy. ***You love being a woman!***

## CHAKRA TWO - NOT IN YOUR POWER

***When you are not in your power in this center you are disconnected from your own emotions and needs, while at the same time you are aware of and may even absorbing or taking on responsibility for other people's emotions.*** You emotionally react from your little girl energy often (because you are unaware of your unmet needs or hurts from childhood) instead of responding from your empowered woman self. You are easily knocked off balance by your emotions because you don't know how to work through painful emotions when you are triggered or because you do not take responsibility for them. Instead, you may criticize, judge, complain, or blame others for feeling the way you do. You can stay stuck in your painful emotions rather than processing and transforming them.

You do not have healthy emotional or sexual boundaries. You may have sex with someone because they want to, not because it's the right time for you and what you actually want. Instead of feeling that your body, sensuality, and sexuality are beautiful and sacred, you may feel a sense of disconnection from or shame about them. You disconnect from, deny, or devalue your feminine energy and may even see it as weak, but view your masculine energy as strong.

## AWAKENING AND EMBRACING YOUR EMPOWERED FEMININE ENERGY

Everything in this book will help you awaken and embrace your empowered feminine energy, but in this section, you will be learning how to do this with specific empowered woman practices for chakra two.

In chapter one I shared that one way of helping you to stay grounded was to bring a part of your awareness into your body, especially the lower half of your body, your legs and feet at different times throughout the day.

In this chapter, with this secret, I'm inviting you to bring your awareness into chakra two (about 2-3 inches below your navel and inside the center of your pelvis) whenever you can remember to do it throughout the day. Believe it or not, when you focus a part of your awareness there, it increases your empowered feminine energy presence and helps you to feel more balanced and centered. Specifically bringing your attention to your second chakra will also help you to be more in touch with your emotions and help you to create that inner sense of safety and security we discussed with secret one. The reason is that your body feels safe when you are emotionally home and present to yourself in this chakra. You will also feel more self-confident.

*The main organ in your pelvis, your uterus, is like a woman's second heart.* Studies have shown that many prescription medications have similar effects on both the heart in your chest and the heart in your womb. This is because the muscles of these two important organs are similar. Both the heart in your chest and the heart in your pelvis are two of your empowered feminine energy activation points. There is a powerful connection between your second and fourth chakras (your two hearts). Even if you no longer have a uterus or you are in menopause, this powerful energy connection still exists.

*To assist you in being physically and emotionally present in your second chakra, think of yourself as a queen and your second chakra as your throne.* Imagine that whenever you have a part of your awareness there, it's like you are seated on your queen's throne. You will feel a sense of "I am emotionally present to myself first and then to others; I am here; I am home." This will help you strengthen your emotional boundaries and not absorb the stressful or negative emotions of others or the environment. It will help you to be more aware of your emotions and needs, and it will help you to have a more magnetic and attractive empowered feminine energy presence.

*In addition, when you're present in your body, you will naturally be more in touch with your sensuality, meaning you will have the ability to enjoy the pleasure of all of your senses.* Everything you are seeing, hearing, tasting, touching, and feeling is all part of having a body and being alive. As an empowered woman you want to embrace all of your senses and appreciate all of the enjoyment you can experience with your physical body. For example, when was the last time you "stopped to smell the roses?" If you're not present in your body and your focus is in your head all the time, you won't be aware of your senses and all of the pleasure you can experience through them.

## SEXUAL BOUNDARIES

In addition to having emotional boundaries, so you don't absorb other people's emotions and feel exhausted or drained, you also want to have boundaries when it comes to your sexual energy. In other words, you want to be clear on what kind of person, under what circumstances, and in what kind of relationship you are willing to share this deep, intimate part of yourself. Think of your sexuality as something very precious and sacred, just like your entire body. As an empowered woman, you don't just let anyone have access to this deep and sacred part of you.

While healthy sexuality is beyond the scope of this book, there are plenty of wonderful books out there on the topic of sex, including some for women who have gone through menopause, which doesn't have to mark the end of a healthy, happy sex life. For example, you may want to explore tantra, a practice that brings together spirituality and sexuality with an emphasis on energy, connection, and emotional intimacy.

## CREATIVITY

Creativity is also a big aspect of chakra two. Your life force energy is your creative energy. It is what enables you to create a new life inside your body. Own and acknowledge that you are a powerful, creative woman whether or not you have actually given birth to a child. We as women can give birth to many things. Writing and publishing a book such as this is giving birth to a creative project! Women are naturally very creative, so please pay attention to your heart's desires and longings and what it is that you want to create in your life. More on this in chapter four.

### PRACTICES TO AWAKEN YOUR EMPOWERED FEMININE ENERGY

As mentioned earlier, you have empowered feminine energy throughout your whole body, but chakra two is where this energy is stored. *Even though you might have a feminine energy essence at your core, you may be somewhat disconnected from it or out of touch with it for the reasons we discussed in the empowered woman principles section of this book.* The following practices will help you to awaken and embrace your empowered feminine energy if needed or desired. If you feel you have been out of balance and in your masculine energy most of the time, these practices will help you to get back into balance, which can improve your overall health, as well as the health your female organs. In addition, they can also increase your attractiveness to empowered masculine energy men or people who are in their empowered masculine energy because as I mentioned earlier, opposite energies attract.

**1.** Practice bringing your awareness down from your head and your thinking mind into your body, into your feelings and into the present moment. Practice being aware of your emotions and what you are feeling in your heart and in your body. Bring your attention to your breathing and breathe deeply down into your belly often throughout the day. As you breathe, allow your shoulders and chest to relax and your heart to open.

**2.** Imagine a beautiful orange light in the center of your pelvis from time to time. Whenever you are speaking and interacting with others practice having a part of your attention in your second chakra, your feminine power center. You will be more magnetic, more self-confident and people will feel more of an emotional connection with you. You will also stay more in touch with your own emotions. This is an ongoing practice, it's not something that you just do once in a while. Rather than always being in your head thinking (masculine energy), keep practicing being aware of your body and connected to your feelings (feminine energy). Practice sensing what it feels like when you are seated on your queen's throne, at home and present with a part of your awareness in your feminine power center.

**3.** Your sensuality is part of your feminine energy. To get more in touch with your senses try doing things *slower*. Eat slower, put your clothes on and take them off slower than usual. When you start to slow down you will naturally become more grounded and you'll be more in tune with your senses. Become aware of how food tastes as you eat it, how your face feels when you wash it, how your body feels in the shower, how the air smells when it's raining etc. Slowing down will help you get more in touch with your senses and therefore your empowered feminine energy.

**4.** Get to know your three empowered feminine energy activation points.

**The first empowered feminine energy activation point is your heart.** Bring your attention into your heart as often as you can, and have the intention to radiate love. This will activate your feminine energy.

**Your second empowered feminine energy activation point is your second chakra.** All of the practices listed here and everything I discuss in this chapter will help awaken this center and second activation point.

**Your third empowered feminine energy activation point is in the movement of your hips.** Feminine energy is primarily associated with the hips, belly, pelvis and down through your legs and feet, while masculine energy is more associated with the upper chest (above the heart), the shoulders, and out through the arms. One way to awaken your feminine energy is to pay attention to the lower half of your body when you walk. Most women lean forward when they walk and remain focused in their heads thinking about all they have to do. Instead, lean back and drop your attention and energy down from your head into your heart and then down into your hips. Feel your legs as you walk; this too will activate your feminine energy and make you more attractive to men with empowered masculine energy.

**5. Dance is one of the most powerful, beautiful, and enjoyable ways to awaken and embrace your empowered feminine energy, especially forms of dance where you are moving your hips, such as belly dance or salsa**. To begin, simply put on some beautiful slow tempo, flowing kind of music that you like and just start moving to it, slowly circling your hands and arms, rotating your hips, rolling your shoulders, etc. It's also easy and fun to learn basic belly dance movements such as undulations, hip shimmies and snake arms. I've taught these movements and practices to my women clients who are interested, and they find it very enjoyable and empowering. You may even want to buy a pretty veil and twirl around the room with some music on, I promise you that will help you to awaken your empowered feminine energy! I do a few hip shimmies and little dancing and twirling around with my red veil as often as I can!

**6.** Place one hand on your heart and one on your belly as often as you can, tune in and just notice how you're feeling. Ask yourself what could you do today that would bring you joy, nourishment, or pleasure? Dance, a hot bath, a walk in nature? If you have to do something that isn't enjoyable to you, like cleaning or washing the dishes, do something to make it more enjoyable, like putting on some music that you love.

**7. Another thing that gets you more in touch with your empowered feminine energy is relaxing.** When you relax, rest and slow your brainwaves down, your nervous system also relaxes and calms down, which then helps your heart to open. As your heart opens, it helps your nervous system to relax, and this creates a beautiful healing cycle. Take some time to rest, breathe deep and listen to some beautiful music. Any kind of music that touches and opens your heart awakens your empowered feminine energy.

**8. Practicing a relaxing form of yoga is very good for helping you to connect with your body and your empowered feminine energy.** As you do the stretches, you can repeat mantras that help you feel however you want to feel, such as beautiful, peaceful, worthy or powerful. I call this "moving mantra meditation," and recommend it to my clients who don't like to sit still in meditation.

**9. Connecting with and opening your heart helps you connect with love and your empowered feminine energy.** Whatever you're doing during the day, *consciously do it with love*, even if you're just combing your hair, do it with love. Consciously send love to your body, to yourself, to other people. Also, practice *receiving* which is feminine energy. Allow a man to open a door for you, carry some groceries, help you, or do things for you. Allow yourself to fully receive compliments from people. Receiving requires an open heart. Practice being grateful, gratitude opens your heart.

**10. Empowered feminine energy is associated with light as well as love, Divine Love and Divine Light.** I'm not saying that there is no darkness, because there certainly is. We have both the sun and the moon, day and night, joyful emotions and painful emotions. I am talking about the *radiance* of your empowered feminine energy.

**Empowered feminine energy expresses itself as radiance and light.** That is why we sometimes say a pregnant woman or a woman in love *glows*. When you awaken and embrace your feminine energy you become more radiant. You glow. You will be more magnetic and attractive. You as a woman are a divine embodiment of love and light. You just need to *become aware of what has been dimming your light*, so you can allow your light to fully shine, **which is ultimately what you are learning throughout this book.**

A very important aspect of allowing your light to shine and of embracing your empowered feminine energy is learning how to **master your emotions.**

## MASTERING YOUR EMOTIONS

There are several reasons why many women are not fully present and in their power in their second chakra. For example, *it might be because you grew up in a chaotic or unstable environment where you felt anxious often.* As a result, you might have become very busy tuning in to everyone else's feelings around you in order to help you feel safe. At the same time, you were losing an emotional connection with yourself and your own feelings. This is how codependence begins. Codependency is really a loss of connection with yourself, because for various reasons you weren't able to form a healthy sense of self as a child. There is also a negative self-concept underneath codependency. Self-esteem, codependency and setting healthy boundaries will be discussed in the next chapter, with secret number three. For now, we are focusing specifically on your emotions, but of course all of your chakras are interconnected.

*As an empowered woman you have emotional boundaries.* You don't absorb and take responsibility for other peoples' emotions. Other people may trigger you emotionally, but you know that you are responsible for your own emotions and not the emotions of others. As the master of your emotions, you want to be responding most of the time instead of reacting. Examples of reacting are when you say things you wish you hadn't said, when you're avoiding, numbing, repressing your emotions, shutting down, drowning in your feelings, or when you're blaming, projecting on, or criticizing others. It's when you are not coming from love, and that won't feel good to you or to others.

## EMOTIONS ARE ENERGETIC MESSENGERS

*Emotions are energy in motion and they are experienced as feelings in your body.* It was once thought that when we experienced an emotion it was only happening in our brain. Science has since proven that when we feel an emotion, we actually feel it throughout our whole body. However, each specific emotion affects a certain part of your brain and often a specific part of your body. Chinese medicine has known this for a long time. For example, unresolved grief will often affect your lungs and unhappiness with your work can affect your heart. We're all human so we all emotionally react rather than respond with love from time to time. This usually comes from unhealed hurts from the past and the little girl energy inside of you, or from the current stress and challenges you are facing, so rather than judge yourself, have compassion for yourself. Since our culture has discounted and devalued feminine energy (including emotions) for so many years, you may judge yourself for having "negative" emotions, the same way you may judge and criticize your body.

*In addition, since many of our parents did not know or learn how to master their own emotions, most of us did not have very good role models when growing up.* It may not have even been okay for you to express your emotions at all. Although you don't want to stay stuck or drown in your painful emotions, you also don't want to make yourself wrong for having them. You want to allow yourself to feel them and understand their messages, so you can release or reprogram them. More on reprogramming in chapters three and six.

*Look at your emotions as a beautiful and sacred part of being a woman.* When I write or talk about emotions, I usually don't refer to them as negative or positive because calling them negative or positive may cause you to judge yourself for having the "negative" ones. The reality is you have painful emotions and you have pleasant, uplifting emotions. Many people will say things like, "negative emotions make you sick," which is not true. It's what you do or don't do with your emotions that can cause problems. If you are repressing, stuffing, dwelling on, trying to avoid, or unconsciously projecting or blaming others for your emotions, the result may be energy blockages and toxicity, which can contribute to disease in the body. Yet it's not the emotion itself causing the problems; it's how you are handling them. Instead, you can learn how to master your emotions. Remember, your emotions are energetic messengers. *They are bringing something important to your attention.*

## THREE KEYS TO MASTERING YOUR EMOTIONS

**There are three keys to mastering your emotions. The first is understanding that you are not your emotions**. When you feel a specific emotion, say, "I FEEL sad, rather than, "I AM sad." You are not your sadness or your anger or your fear. There is a part of you that is deeper than your emotions and deeper than your thoughts. Deep inside of you there is a loving presence, a loving essence that is who you really are. This part of you is referred to by many different names such as, your soul, your spirit, your higher self or your consciousness. It is an important part of your empowered woman self. It is the part of you that can observe and become aware of what you are feeling. When you're aware of that deeper part of you, you can allow yourself to feel a painful emotion without emotionally reacting. You are able to choose how you want to respond. And if you are too emotionally upset and triggered to respond instead of react, you can take some time to yourself to work through your emotions before you communicate them to someone else.

The **second key** to mastering your emotions is learning how to feel, understand, process, and transform them. More on this shortly.

The **third key** to mastering your emotions is that you need to complete or be in the process of completing your emotional past. This is associated with your heart chakra and it will be discussed in chapter four. What's important here is that you don't want to be harboring resentments, unforgiveness, and a lot of emotional baggage from the past. The more you learn how to handle your emotions in the present moment, the less emotional baggage you will carry from your past.

The good news is that even though we all have some emotional healing to do, you don't have to dig things up from the past because whatever needs to be processed and healed—unresolved emotions—will be triggered in your current circumstances, especially when you are in an intimate relationship! Or they will come up when you become ill or lose your job, etc. When you really tune in, you often find that your painful emotions are not just about the current experience that you are going through, but they are also often bringing up the same emotions you felt somewhere in your past. For example, if you are experiencing a loss in your life right now, this may also bring up other losses from your past that you never allowed yourself to fully grieve. It all comes up to be healed! Emotions that aren't felt and dealt with don't go away. ***Your emotions are a beautiful and sacred part of being a woman, they are here to guide you with their important messages.***

## EMPOWERED WOMAN EMOTIONAL MASTERY PRACTICE

*Here are three questions to help you feel and understand the messages of your emotions as they come up in your daily life.*

When most people start to feel a painful emotion, they try to avoid it in various ways, but this only buries it. When you are feeling unhappy, not at peace, or you are feeling a painful emotion, bring your attention inside and connect with yourself. Start by placing one hand on your heart and one hand on your belly.

**The first question to ask yourself is, "What am I feeling?"** Perhaps your answer is that you feel anxious or sad. Notice where you feel the emotion in your body. Emotions are physical which is why being present in your body helps you connect with them. Breathe and let the energy of that emotion flow through you, just allowing yourself to feel it. Next name the emotion—fear, sadness, frustration, hurt—and continue to breathe into it and feel it without judging yourself in any way.

**The second question you want to ask yourself is, "What am I needing?"** Underneath a painful emotion is usually an unmet need and/or a false belief. It may be an emotional need coming from your adult self or from your inner little girl who had needs that were not met as a child. If you are feeling anger, there may be a need for you to set a boundary. Perhaps you are feeling anxious, and when you ask yourself what you are needing, the answer might be that you need comfort. This need may be coming from your adult woman self, your inner little girl or both. There may be a false belief or repetitive negative thought pattern connected with your emotion. More on that later in this chapter.

**The third question is, "What loving action can I take to meet this need?"** or, **"What would be the most loving thing I can do for myself right now to meet this need?"** Maybe the answer you get is that calling a friend would be comforting, or perhaps praying or meditating. This is how you love yourself emotionally. You are present with yourself, you are aware of your feelings, and you attend to your emotional needs. Most women emotionally abandon themselves when they have a painful emotion instead of loving and connecting with themselves. You can emotionally abandon yourself in many different ways—stuffing your feelings with food, staying super busy, drinking too much, blaming other people, or criticizing and judging yourself for having painful emotions in the first place.

Instead, as an empowered woman, become curious about your painful emotions and what they are trying to tell you. What is the unmet need underneath the emotion? With loneliness for example, there is a need for more connection, either with yourself, with other people or with your Spiritual Source. When you hold a loving space for your emotions, you will be better able to understand their messages. Practice being grounded and present in your second chakra and tuning in to how you're feeling and what you're needing as you go through your day. In chapter four you will learn more about tuning in to what you are desiring, which is more connected to your heart, but in this second center, chakra two, it's about your emotional needs.

## REPARENTING YOUR INNER CHILD

*The way your parents loved you and handled your emotions is how you learned to love and treat yourself emotionally*. If you had emotional needs that weren't met when you were a little girl—and since none of our parents were perfect—I would say this is the case for the majority of women—then what you need to do now is become your own unconditionally loving, emotionally present parent. You need to be a loving mother to the little girl inside of you, validating and understanding her feelings. You need to attend to her emotional needs. Believe it or not, reparenting your inner child helps you to master your emotions, because you will be better able to respond from your empowered woman adult self, rather than react from the past hurts of your younger self.

Reparenting your younger self is important because when you love and treat yourself emotionally the way your parents loved and treated you when you were a child, then as an adult, you will often attract the same kind of treatment and energy from other people. For example, if one of your parents was critical of you or abandoned you emotionally, you then learn to do the same thing to yourself. That's what needs to change (how you are treating yourself) because if it doesn't you will likely attract people into your life who criticize you and are emotionally unavailable. In other words, even when you forgive your parents for their shortcomings (this is not about blaming them, they did the best they could), the other half of the healing and transformation is healing and transforming the relationship that you now have with yourself. ***It is learning how to love yourself in the ways that you needed and wanted to be loved as a child and in the ways that you need and want to be loved now as an adult. This includes being emotionally present to yourself and taking care of your emotional needs.***

You want to be sure that you're not trying to get a partner to be the parent you never had but always wanted, now that you're an adult. It's really up to you to be your own unconditionally loving parent to yourself now. Have compassion for the little girl inside of you that perhaps didn't always get important needs met when you were younger. No one else can reparent that little girl inside of you the way you can. You will have difficulty being an empowered woman if your hurt or scared inner little girl (in your subconscious mind) is emotionally reacting all the time and running the show. Again, becoming her loving parent will help you to respond from your empowered woman self when you are emotionally triggered.

**EMPOWERED WOMAN PRACTICE - LEARNING TO MOTHER YOURSELF**

When you become aware of a hurt or fear coming up from the little girl inside of you, it's the perfect opportunity for you to learn how to be a loving mother to yourself. First, validate and have compassion for your inner child's feelings. Next, tell her what the truth is. For example, if you notice that you're feeling unimportant and unloved because your boyfriend is not calling you as much as he usually does, ask yourself if this feeling could also be coming from past experiences that you had as a child. If so, tell the inner child part of yourself that you know and understand that she is feeling unimportant and unloved - *and* at the same time, tell her that the truth is she is very important and very much loved both by you and by your boyfriend. He is just very busy with work and the reason he has been calling less often has nothing to do with her. In other words, you help this younger part of you to release and replace her painful feelings (feeling unloved and unimportant), with the exact opposite feelings - ***feeling loved and important!***

In this example, the original cause for the painful feelings of your inner child might be that your father did not spend much time with you because of his work. If so, you likely internalized that, took it personally and thought his lack of attention meant that you *weren't important or loved*. It is also likely that no one ever told you the truth (that his lack of attention had nothing to do with you), to help you not take it personally, *but you can do that for yourself now.* Your empowered woman self can reparent and mother your inner child and tell her the truth, that her father's behavior in the past and your boyfriend's behavior in the current time, does not mean that you are unloved and unimportant.

***Reparenting your inner child is really reprogramming your subconscious mind, because your core subconscious programming comes from the first 6 or 7 years of your life.*** You will learn more about reprogramming your subconscious mind with secrets three and six. You can also share your feelings with your boyfriend and tell him what you want and would love, (perhaps a daily phone call for example) but *how* you communicate your feelings is very important. You will learn about empowered loving communication with secret five. And if over time you are not being treated with the importance and love that you want and deserve, you can decide whether or not your boyfriend is the right partner for you!

## APPRECIATING YOUR EMOTIONAL VULNERABILTIY

Think about what it would be like if we didn't have emotions. Without them, you wouldn't be human; you would be like a robot or a computer. Emotions give us a sense of depth and humanness; they are a part of our healthy vulnerability as women. Healthy vulnerability is connected to your emotional needs therefore it is an aspect of chakra two and part of your empowered feminine energy. Healthy vulnerability is not weak, as society may try to tell you. Fortunately, there are now experts like Brene Brown who have written books on the power of vulnerability. The reality is, it actually takes a lot of strength to allow yourself to be vulnerable. More on healthy vulnerability in chapter five.

We're not talking here about the kind of vulnerability that is being naïve and letting yourself get taken advantage of because that is a woman who is in her disempowered feminine energy, one who doesn't know how to set boundaries or is not in tune with her feelings and intuition. As an empowered woman, you are very aware of and connected to your emotions and you allow yourself to feel them. *You embrace the beauty of your healthy vulnerability, which is having an open heart and being emotionally authentic*.

You can allow certain people to see some of the feelings that you have, not everyone of course, but certain trustworthy people. If you have put up walls up around your heart and you are not letting yourself be vulnerable, it will prevent you from developing meaningful relationships with others. Having emotions and being in touch with your needs and vulnerability is not weak; it's actually a sign of emotional maturity, emotional intelligence, and strength, and it is what allows you to have intimate connections with other people. *There is no intimacy without vulnerability, and there is no empathy without vulnerability. To be able to empathize with what someone else is going through you have to be in touch with your own vulnerability, which means being in touch with your emotions and needs.*

Ultimately what you want to do with your painful emotions is allow yourself to feel them, understand their messages, and then process and transform them. Transformation doesn't mean that you transcend and rise above them or that you don't feel them. It means that you allow yourself to feel your emotions and because of that, you learn, heal, or grow in some way. You change the emotional pain into something beneficial, and you grow in love and wisdom. This prevents your emotional energy from being stuck in your body, which can contribute to both health and relationship problems. Sometimes just validating your feelings, having self-compassion, and being present with yourself when you are feeling emotional pain helps the emotion to dissipate or release. If you instead resist a painful emotion, it will often persist.

Let's take a look now at the main categories of painful emotions and how to process and transform them, starting with fear.

## EMPOWERED WOMAN PRACTICES FOR TRANSFORMING EMOTIONS

**Fear** - You ultimately want to transform fear into feelings of peace, trust, love, safety, courage, or faith. All emotions have messages. Fear is often like a warning system telling you to pay attention. It might be telling you that there is something you need to do or not do, such as don't walk down that dark alley by yourself. Healthy fear is there to help protect you and you want to listen to its message. But you may have other fears that are just keeping you awake at night worrying or prohibiting you from making the changes that you want to make or that are keeping you from opening your heart. These are fears you want to face and transform.

In other words, your fear is either telling you that you need to pay attention to something and listen to its guidance (healthy fear), or it could be an unhealthy fear that's getting in the way of something that you really need to do that is good for your soul's expansion and growth. It is up to you to say, "Yes, I'm afraid, but I'm going to do this anyway, because when I listen to my heart and soul, this feels like what I need to do."

The more you practice tuning in to your feelings, the more you will understand the specific message of your fear. You might find that praying or meditating helps you release fear and cultivate inner peace. You can also use your breath to release the energy of fear whenever you exhale. As you breathe out, affirm that you are releasing the energy of fear from your body and your mind. Connect with your heart and repeat a mantra or affirmation that brings you a sense of peace, love or safety. In other words, you can transform and release fear and train your brain to calm down with the power of your breath, your mind and by connecting with your heart. You can also transform fear by connecting with your Spiritual Source through prayer or meditation. Yoga or other forms of movement and exercise can also help you release worry and unhealthy fear.

**Anxiety – Anxiety is often the result of avoiding and pushing down other emotions.** Although fear and anxiety can overlap and both produce a similar fight or flight stress response in the body, there is a difference between the two. As with fear, with anxiety you want to transform anxiety into a sense of peace and safety. With fear, there is usually a known threat to your safety, security or survival. With anxiety, there can be a vague sense of apprehension in response to an unknown threat. There's usually an uneasiness about the possibility of something bad happening or of being harmed. To heal and transform anxiety often requires learning how to feel and process core emotions such as fear, sadness and anger. Many people with anxiety have experienced some kind of trauma in their life. **Please reach out for support if needed to heal and transform your anxiety. There are many skilled trauma healing therapists who can help.**

**Sadness and Grief** - The message sadness often brings is that this is the time for you to let go of someone or something. It may be that someone or something is no longer for your highest good, and you have a choice as to whether you want to let it or them go. For example, you may stay in a relationship too long because you're afraid to be alone. When you do let go, you will feel sadness, but if you allow yourself to feel it, it will eventually be transformed into a new life or a new relationship.

**The emotion of grief is much deeper than sadness. It's a more intense emotion because you don't have a choice about letting go, it is an irretrievable loss.** With grief you must eventually find a way to accept the loss that can't be changed, for example when a loved one passes away. Grief is intense and deep, and there are specific stages you must go through as you heal. Grief usually involves feeling many different emotions such as anger, fear, sadness, guilt or regret. One of the things that can really help is to talk with other people who are going through similar losses such as in a grief and loss support group. Allow yourself to cry and let the tears flow, because they are the best way to release sadness and grief. You can also release grief through writing and with various forms of creative expression and music.

After a period of healing, grief often transforms and changes us and can cause us to feel a tremendous sense of gratitude. Very often we don't appreciate something or someone until we have lost it or them, so grief can teach us to be more grateful and appreciative of people, places and things, or life itself when we experience a loss.

**Depression**- Depression is a normal and natural stage in the grief process. If you are not grieving a loss, then similar to anxiety, **depression can be a sign that you may be avoiding or pushing down (de-pressing) core emotions such as fear, anger or sadness.** To transform depression, it can be very helpful to learn how to feel and process all of your emotions. Again, as with anxiety, you may need to heal trauma from your past. **Reach out for a trauma healing therapist for support if needed.**

Underneath depression there are often feelings of hopelessness and despair. I've also noticed that beneath depression there is usually something that needs to "die." By die I mean something that needs to change and transform within yourself or in your life. For example, what needs to "die" or change could be an unhealthy relationship pattern of yours or the way you talk to and treat yourself. **As you heal and transform depression, you will begin to feel a sense of hope and joy again.**

**Loneliness:** Loneliness is telling you that you need to feel more connected—to yourself, other people, or to your Spiritual Source. It is possible to feel lonely around people or in a relationship. Explore and become aware of what kind of connection you need and want. Do you spend too much time alone and need more human connection and interaction? Or is it that you have plenty of interaction with someone or others, but no emotional intimacy? Become aware of your emotional needs, what's missing, and then take action to meet your needs and fulfill your desires.

**Guilt**: There are two kinds of guilt, healthy, appropriate guilt and unhealthy, inappropriate guilt. Healthy guilt reminds you that you did something that went against your moral compass or your integrity or that you did something that doesn't feel good to you, so you therefore feel bad about it. What will help transform guilt is self-forgiveness, making amends to someone, apologizing, and changing your behavior.

Unhealthy, inappropriate guilt is when you feel guilty because you are taking on responsibility that is not yours. It's being overly responsible for other people or situations and is a part of codependency and low self-esteem. You may feel guilty about something that you had no control over, but yet you blame yourself and feel like it is your fault when the reality is it's not your fault at all. If this sounds familiar to you, you'll want to release any unhealthy, inappropriate guilt by checking in and asking yourself if the guilt you are feeling is really appropriate or if you are taking on responsibility that is not yours.

The way you transform unhealthy guilt is by learning how to have boundaries and increasing your self-esteem which we'll discuss more in chapter three. If you haven't had good healthy boundaries with people until now and you start to set them, you may have to face the fear of having people disapprove of you and your choices. But the good news is that when you remain true to yourself, despite their disapproval and perhaps their attempt to try to get you to take on the unhealthy guilt, you will be well on your way to becoming a more empowered woman!

**Shame:** With guilt you feel bad about something you did; with shame you feel bad about who you are at your core. This is self-esteem and self-worth at its lowest. When you feel bad about who you are, you may feel that you are not good enough, flawed in some way, unlovable or unworthy. What heals and transforms shame is increasing your self-esteem, self-love and self-compassion, and we'll be discussing this in the next two chapters.

**Regret:** Regret is when you look back at your past and wish that you had made a different choice. The way to release and transform regret is to first of all forgive yourself and remind yourself that you did the best you were able to do with the information and consciousness you had at the time. Second, ask yourself what you learned through the experience. What did you learn and how did you grow because of the decision or choice that you made? The answers to these two questions will help you release the regret and transform your pain into acceptance and peace.

**Anger:** Anger can often be a cover for more vulnerable feelings that you have underneath, such as hurt or sadness. Tune in and if that is the case, then you want to get more in touch with your vulnerability and allow yourself to feel the hurt, sadness, loss, or fear that's hidden under the anger. *Anger can also very often be a message that you need to set a boundary.* You will learn about boundaries with secrets three and five. In addition to setting healthy boundaries, you can often release anger with movement and exercise, with various forms of creative expression and music, journaling, talking about it or expressing it in a healthy way to another person.

Ultimately, to completely release anger, you need transform anger into *forgiveness*. Healthy anger in the moment is fine. It can jumpstart healing, but if anger becomes stuck and is not fully released, then it becomes resentment. Resentment is not healthy, and it can very often cause energy blockages and contribute to disease in your body. It can also prevent you from moving forward and making the changes that you want in your relationships and life. Forgiveness is connected to your heart chakra. We'll discuss forgiveness with secret four in chapter four.

## THE CONNECTION BETWEEN EMOTIONS AND BELIEFS

The interesting thing with emotions is that they may also be connected with your thoughts and beliefs (you will learn more about beliefs in chapter three). However, sometimes an emotion is not connected to a belief and you really need to allow yourself to just feel it. Take grief for example. There's nothing you can do to heal grief but to feel it and go through it, and reach out for support if needed. It's not about your beliefs; it's about feeling and riding the waves of all of your emotions.

Quite often, when you allow yourself to feel and transform an emotion, you may find that you're able to think more positively or perceive things differently. Other times you may find yourself having a repetitive emotion over and over, because it's an emotional pattern you've likely had for years in your subconscious mind. Ask yourself, "What are the thought patterns and beliefs going through my mind when I'm feeling this emotion?" For example, the anger you are feeling might be coming up because you are believing that you are powerless to change anything in your life. If you change your thinking and choose a different belief, such as the belief that you *do* have the power to change your circumstances for the better, then you may notice that you no longer feel angry.

In other words, sometimes when you shift you're thinking and change what you're believing, your painful emotion will release and you feel better, but not always. As I mentioned earlier, recent studies have shown that your heart communicates more with your brain than the other way around, which is why changing your thinking doesn't always work to help you feel better emotionally. Please reach out for the appropriate emotional support and professional help if and when needed.

A lot of people think that their thoughts control their emotions and so they are trying to think positive, but it doesn't work for them if they are *feeling* pain or hurt on the inside. Very often it's our emotions that are controlling our thoughts. For example, have you ever noticed that when you fall in love with someone, your emotions cause you to think only positive thoughts about them? And if you're angry with someone, you will usually see and think more about their faults and the things that you don't like about them. In my experience, *I have seen that when my clients are able to shift their emotional state, it changes how they think and what they believe, in other words, it helps to transforms their mind!*

Yes, emotions are there for a reason and they have important messages for you. You definitely want to listen to the messages of your painful emotions and attend to your emotional needs, as well as look the connection between your emotions and your thoughts and beliefs. But if you notice that you have a chronic, repetitive, painful emotional pattern, changing it will usually require utilizing the power of uplifting emotions, not just your thoughts. *It is possible to program into your subconscious mind how you actually want to feel, thus changing both your emotional state and your mental state (your thinking and your beliefs) at the same time.*

You will learn how to do this and with secrets three and six.

## MASTERING YOUR EMOTIONS SUMMARY

To summarize, you have so many different emotions and you want to allow yourself to feel them without judgement, yet at the same time you don't want to get stuck in them or drown in them. You want to learn how to shift your painful, repetitive emotional states, program your subconscious mind with uplifting emotions and practice consciously *choosing how you want to feel*. This is part of mastering your emotions. It's not black and white with emotions which is why so many people don't want to deal with them. They are complex, and we are complex human beings. You don't want to harbor old painful emotions in your body that can cause energy blockages and keep you stuck in painful relationship patterns.

You also want to observe what you are thinking in your mind when you are feeling a difficult emotion. Notice if changing your thoughts or a belief can help you shift from a painful to a more uplifting emotional state. For example, if you are feeling hopeless often, you may be believing that what you want is not possible. You can then work on changing that belief. With guilt you may have the belief that it is wrong for you to have what you want or that you are responsible for your another's happiness, which, of course, is not true. With shame, you are often believing something that is completely false, which is that you are not worthy or good enough. ***Beliefs, thoughts and emotions are all so interconnected!***

Or you may want to work on changing your emotional state first, which may then help you to change your false beliefs and negative thought patterns, with the end result being that you may no longer feel the painful emotion. The more uplifted you feel emotionally, the easier it will be to think positive thoughts. Often a combination of both approaches is needed when working with your emotions. Learning how to master your emotions is quite an art and an ongoing process, so please be patient and compassionate with yourself. ***If you keep practicing what you learned in this chapter and in the coming chapters, you will be well on your way to becoming a more empowered woman in love and in life.***

**SECRET TWO SUMMARY**

**How Being in Your Power in Chakra Two Helps You to Create the Healthy Love and Life You Want and Deserve**

**Health:** Being in your masculine energy most of the time and disconnected from your feminine energy creates an imbalance which can negatively affect your health, especially the health of your female organs. Awakening and embracing your empowered feminine energy can help to balance your hormones and bring healing to your whole body. Getting in touch with and embracing your creativity, sensuality, and sexuality is also known to have beneficial effects on your health. Being able to master your emotions and process painful emotions is very good for your health because repressed emotional energy creates energy blockages in your body which can then contribute to disease, problems with sleep, excess weight or physical pain. Utilizing the power of elevated, uplifting emotions can help your body to relax and heal and help you to think more positively and transform your mind.

**Love and Relationships**: Awakening and embracing your empowered feminine energy helps you increase your self-confidence and enjoy being a woman. It helps you become more loving and comfortable with your body, sensuality, sexuality, and your feelings in your intimate relationships. You will be more connected to your creative power and in touch with your emotions and your intuition, both of which help you to make healthy and wise relationship decisions. Awakening and embracing your empowered feminine energy can increase your attractiveness to empowered masculine energy people or men. Being emotionally present to yourself and being able to master your emotions are vital components for being in your power in your relationships, because you will be able to respond emotionally from your empowered woman self, instead of reacting from your hurt or fearful inner little girl self. This will help you to resolve conflicts or disagreements sooner and help you to gain more clarity about what is best for you in your relationships.

## CHAKRA TWO EMPOWERED WOMAN MANTRAS

*I awaken and embrace my empowered feminine energy.*

*I am emotionally present to myself and then to others.*

*I allow myself to feel all of my emotions.*

*I am emotionally balanced and centered.*

*I know what I'm feeling and what I'm needing.*

*I take loving action to fulfill my emotional needs.*

*I embrace my passion and creativity.*

*I have healthy emotional and sexual boundaries.*

*I release and transform my painful emotions into love and wisdom.*

*I am able to respond with love rather than react with fear when emotionally triggered.*

*I am the master of my emotions.*

*I have the power to choose how I want to feel.*

*I radiate my own unique form of empowered feminine energy and beauty.*

*I enjoy my body, sensuality, and sexuality.*

*I love being a woman!*

# EMPOWERED WOMAN
# **SECRET THREE**

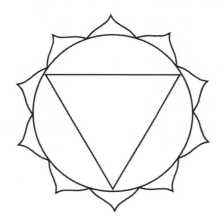

# CHAKRA THREE

*Increasing Your Self-Confidence and Self-Esteem, Changing False Beliefs and Creating Healthy Boundaries and Standards*

# CHAPTER THREE
# SECRET THREE

The third empowered woman secret to creating the healthy love and life you want and deserve corresponds with the third energy center in your body. Chakra three is located in your solar plexus area (the area between the bottom of your breast bone or ribs and your navel) and its color is yellow like that of a bright sun. This chakra is about your personal power, boundaries, self-confidence and self-worth.

In the last chapter you began learning about the connection between your beliefs and emotions. In this chapter you will be learning more about this connection and how to begin changing your subconscious false beliefs to align with your conscious desires. This will give you the ability to create what you want in love and in life with less struggle and more ease. You will also be learning about the importance of having healthy boundaries and standards and how to increase your self-confidence and self-esteem.

## CHAKRA THREE - IN YOUR POWER

When you are in your power in chakra three, you feel a sense of personal power and self-confidence that comes from within. In other words, you are not interested in controlling and having power over others, nor do you feel that other people have power over you. Instead you empower yourself from within. You believe in yourself and feel worthy of having what you truly want. You have high self-esteem and a positive self-concept. You become aware of and change false beliefs and disempowering behavior patterns. You're willing to do the inner work of reparenting your inner child or reprogramming your subconscious mind. When you are in your power in this chakra, you have a healthy sense of self. You have healthy boundaries and standards, and you understand the difference between healthy boundaries and needy expectations.

## CHAKRA THREE - NOT IN YOUR POWER

If you are not in your power in this center you will tend to have low self-esteem, a negative self-concept, and a lack of self-confidence. You may have needy expectations with others rather than healthy boundaries, or you have a difficult time setting boundaries and settle for less than you want and deserve in your relationships. You may feel powerless to make the changes you want in your relationships and life and you try to control or change other people. You might be stuck in unhealthy or unfulfilling relationship patterns. You may be controlled by lifelong, painful, repetitive emotions and false, limiting beliefs in your subconscious mind.

Let's begin by discussing self-confidence, self-esteem, and self-concept. While they are all interconnected, they are worth defining separately.

## SELF-CONFIDENCE, SELF-CONCEPT AND SELF-ESTEEM

**Self-confidence** is about your belief in your abilities. It's a feeling of self-trust and the way you perceive your capability to handle or do something effectively. You may be confident in one situation, but not another. For example, perhaps you are confident that you can teach a specific class, but you are not confident that you can solve a computer problem. In general, it's a feeling that you can attract and have what you want, a state of being and a knowing that you are enough just as you are.

An empowered, self-confident woman does not settle for less than she feels she deserves. She has boundaries and self-respect and is able to walk away from a relationship, job, or other situation that does not feel good to her.

**Your self-concept** is how you perceive yourself overall and in general. It's what you predominately think, feel and believe about yourself in different aspects of your life. It may not be the same for every area of your life. For example, it might be positive for your career, but negative as far as relationships go. The primary practice for changing your self-concept is self-love. Loving yourself can include reparenting your inner child, reprogramming your subconscious mind, and changing the negative thoughts, perceptions and feelings that you have about yourself.

**Self-esteem** is deeper than self-confidence and more specific than your self-concept. Someone can be very self-confident in their abilities and very successful in the outer world, yet deep inside have low self-esteem. Self-esteem is about *how you feel about who you are.* Unlike your overall perception of yourself (self-concept), self-esteem specifically has to do with your perception and feelings about your overall *worth and value.* With low self-esteem, you may feel unworthy, undeserving, not good enough, flawed in some way, or unlovable. These feelings most often come from false beliefs and painful emotional patterns in the subconscious mind from early childhood experiences when you took everything that was happening around you personally.

## YOUR WORTHINESS IS WITHIN

Unfortunately, most women are taught to define their worth externally, feeling worthy only if they meet certain requirements. They attach their worth to how much they weigh or other aspects of their physical appearance such as their age. They may also define themselves by whether or not a particular man wants to commit to them or not. These things have nothing to do with your worthiness as a woman. If you define your worth externally, you are giving your power away. *Your worthiness and power are within.*

The only thing that you need to do to be a worthy, valuable woman is to be born and exist. Your worth is innate. It is not dependent on external things that can change such as your body, your age, your job, or whether a partner wants to be with you or not. You are giving your power away when you allow another person, the media, and/or outer experiences and situations to determine your worth. No one can take your worthiness away from you, but you can give it away, which means that you are the one that can decide to take it back. You can decide to claim and define your own worth from within.

*As an empowered woman you know that your worth has already been established by the Divine. You know that your worth comes from your heart and your unique soul essence.* You're like a rare jewel. There is no one else on the planet that has your unique soul essence, there never has been and there never will be—isn't that amazing? Even if you share a specific quality with someone else such as being compassionate, you are still completely unique because no one else will *express* that compassion *the way you do.* Your worth comes from your unique soul essence and the loving energy of your heart and beautiful spirit.

As you embrace your unique, essential goodness and your intrinsic worth, you will gain a sense of personal power and be able to joyfully express who you really are – your authentic true self! Connecting with your heart and practicing self-love will change your self-concept and raise your self-esteem. Connecting with your Spiritual Source will help you remember the truth of who you really are—*a beautiful, unique soul and spirit who always has been and always will be a worthy, high-value woman.*

## YOU ARE WORTHY AND GOOD ENOUGH RIGHT NOW

*Having coached thousands of women, I have found that a lack of self-love and self-worth are at the root of just about every problem or challenge that women experience.* Far too many women are critical and hard on themselves. A lot of women have an image of perfection in their minds and constantly compare themselves to others or what they think the perfect version of themselves is or should be. If you fall into this trap, you will constantly feel like you are lacking and not good enough.

When you compare yourself negatively to others or to a version of you in the past (when you were younger, thinner, etc.), you will constantly feel the need to change something about yourself such as, your appearance, your personality, your weight, your job, etc. to be worthy of having what you desire.

You may also judge yourself when you feel painful emotions or experience life challenges. You might feel like you have to be perfect to be loved. When you do not feel good enough for the kind of man or for the life you desire, when you feel that you have to change who you are because deep down there is something wrong with you, it will be much harder for you to attract or create what you want in love and life. *It's great to want to make changes, as long as you are making those changes from an unconditionally loving place. This means you feel worthy of what you want, right now as you are, before making those changes in yourself.*

## IT'S ALL ABOUT ENERGY

Women often criticize themselves about their appearance. The truth is that you will attract men, other people, and even career opportunities based on your energy. Energy is everything, as we discussed in the introduction of this book. Your energy includes how you feel about yourself, and that is going to determine how other people, men and potential partners feel about you. It's not about looking or being perfect or saying the perfect things. It's about feeling deep down to the core of your being that who you are is enough and that you are worthy just as you are.

With this sense of self-worth, you can attract the people and experiences you want no matter what you look like, how tall you are, how much you weigh, what kind of hair you have, what you're wearing that day, etc. You can meet men, potential friends, or even clients anywhere and at any time when you are feeling good about yourself on the inside.

*Research has shown that the number one thing men find attractive in a woman is her smile! This is because your smile reveals your energy and how you feel about yourself.*

## CHANGING YOUR SUBCONSCIOUS MIND

Any time you have a thought, neurons (brain cells) fire and release what are called biophotons. Biophotons are photons of light and energy. To make changes in your relationships or life, you very often need to get to the origin of this energy - the emotions and beliefs in your *subconscious mind.*

*There may be times when you want something with your conscious mind, but you're unaware that there are beliefs and emotions in your subconscious mind that are in conflict with your conscious desires.* If you are struggling to manifest the kind of relationship you want or to overcome physical challenges such as extra weight or pain, you may need to explore and change the emotions and beliefs in your subconscious mind. You might have a subconscious block to having what you consciously want. Your subconscious is very tricky and not always easy to understand, but it is always trying to protect you and keep you safe. For example, extra weight is often a subconscious way of protecting yourself when you have a fear of getting hurt in a relationship. It will be hard to lose the extra weight no matter what you eat or how much you exercise if you don't work with the fear of getting hurt in your subconscious mind.

*Although your subconscious mind is always looking for ways to meet your needs for safety and love, it may be running old programs that no longer support you, such as eating to avoid your feelings and gaining weight to protect you from getting hurt.* Everyone's subconscious mind has different blocks and conflicts, unique to them. You may recognize some of your general patterns in this book, but there may be other more specific patterns or blocks that are unique to you.

## THE CHALLENGE WITH HABITUAL THOUGHTS AND FEELINGS

*Your subconscious mind is also the home of your habits.* When self-critical thoughts become habitual they become beliefs. These habitual thought patterns can be hard to change. This has to do with your brain's neural pathways. The easiest way to understand neural pathways is to imagine a big green field of tall grass. If you walk through the grass once, the blades that you step on will pop back up so you don't see a path in the grass. But if you walk that same path several times, the grass in that area will start to flatten and create a path.

***This is the same thing that happens in your mind. You have habitual ways of both thinking and feeling, and it's easy to keep thinking and feeling the same way***. It takes awareness, effort, and practice to create a new neural pathway, a new way of thinking and feeling. A lot of people just try to think positively, hoping to make the changes they want, but this alone seldom works. You also have to change the habitual way you *feel* in your subconscious mind. In other words, for lasting results, you need to change the energy (*both* your thoughts and feelings) in your subconscious mind. Likewise, a lot of people think that just believing they can manifest what they want or believing their body can heal is the key. Yes, *believing is very important,* but healing or manifesting what you want is not just about belief, it also needs to involve ***your heart and your emotions.***

## EMPOWERED WOMAN WORTHY OF LOVE PRACTICE

***Knowing something logically in your head does not change what's in your subconscious mind.*** You must also *feel it* in your body and heart. Here is a practice that can help you change self-critical thoughts that keep you feeling that you are not enough just as you are. Every time you notice yourself thinking or feeling that you're not good enough, first say to yourself silently or out loud with love, "Even with all my imperfections, I am good enough and worthy of what I want ***right now***."

Then, imagine or even find a picture of yourself as a little girl. Look at the picture and notice how worthy she is! Remind yourself that you are still just as worthy of love now as you were then. If you don't have a picture, spend a few moments imagining yourself as a little girl and feeling how lovable you were as a child. To bring those feelings into your heart, place your hand on your heart and feel your worthiness – it is still there. Keep looking at the picture or imagining yourself as a little girl and you will start to *feel it in your heart, rather than just knowing it logically in your head, it is the feeling that will change your subconscious mind.*

## EMPOWERED WOMAN LOVING VOICE PRACTICE

You have a loving voice inside you. It is the voice of your heart and soul, the voice of your *Empowered Woman Within* who always knows the truth about you. This practice will awaken your own loving, empowered woman voice every time you notice you are having any kind of self-critical thought.

Again, place one or both hands on your heart and apologize out loud just like you did with your body and the body-love talk practice in chapter one. Say something like, "I'm so sorry for criticizing you! I love you—you are amazing, beautiful, talented, etc." or whatever it is that you need and want to hear.

Practice connecting often with this part of you. Notice that when you bring your attention into your heart, it is hard to continue criticizing yourself and easier to hear the voice of your soul. As you connect with your heart you will feel more self-love, self-compassion, and self-acceptance. Calling upon your wise, compassionate, *Empowered Woman Within* will transform the energy of your self-critical thoughts and feelings into self-loving thoughts and feelings. *You have the power to do this, it just takes awareness, commitment, and practice!*

## CODEPENDENCY

*Not feeling good enough, low self-esteem, and a lack of self-love greatly contribute to codependency and to giving your power away in relationships.* Codependency comes from not having been able to form a healthy sense of self as a child. This negative self-concept usually comes from blaming yourself when you were a child for not getting the love you needed. Children know when they are not being nurtured or loved the way they need to be, and they will feel like this is their fault which results in a sense of shame. Remember, we internalize everything as children during our first six to seven years of life. Shame, as we discussed in chapter two, is the feeling of, "I'm not okay; something is wrong with me." When you feel unworthy of the love or nurturing you needed as a child and that you still need as an adult, it leads to disempowering codependent relationship patterns—*feeling that you have to earn love, prove your worth, seek approval, people please, over give, and focus on everyone else's feelings and needs but your own, to name just a few!*

## CLAIMING YOUR OWN WORTH AND INCREASING SELF-CONFIDENCE

*You can increase your self-esteem and sense of self-worth, raise your self-confidence and change your energy to align with what you want.* What you consistently think, feel and believe about yourself is in your energy field (your aura) and as previously noted, this is what men and other people feel. I'm not saying that you can never have a negative thought or a painful feeling. But start to become aware of what are you thinking and feeling about yourself throughout your day. Write down your thoughts. When you see your unloving thoughts and false beliefs about yourself on paper, ask yourself, will thinking and believing these things help you to attract and create what you want? If not, know that you can change your thoughts and feelings. You can reprogram your subconscious mind. You will learn how to do this shortly.

As your self-esteem increases and you claim and own your innate worth and value, you will start to feel more self-confident. *True self-confidence is developed by knowing your unique value.* Ask yourself what amazing qualities do you have and in what ways you are unique. Write these attributes down and read them as often as you can. Say them in your mind and *feel them in your heart* before going to sleep. Consistently remind yourself how unique and valuable you truly are. *On a physical level, hold your head up high and sit, stand and walk with good posture, this will also help you to feel more self-confident because how you hold your body affects the way you feel about yourself emotionally. Everything is inter-connected.* This will start to shift your energy and make you more magnetic and attractive to others. Men actually fall in love and stay in love with a woman based on how she feels about herself!

*Remember, your energy is subconsciously communicating to others all the time. You must become aware and conscious of what your energy is communicating, and if it's not communicating what you want, you can change your energy with self-love. Changing your energy with self-love often includes reprogramming the false beliefs you formed in childhood.*

## REPROGRAMMING FALSE BELIEFS

*A belief is something that you choose to accept as true—and you really do have a choice about what you believe.* You can consciously choose what you're going to believe now as an empowered woman instead of allowing your false subconscious beliefs to prevent you from having what you want and deserve.

Regardless of what you have felt, thought or been taught in the past, you are good enough and worthy of having all that your heart desires. It is absolutely possible to release and reprogram your false beliefs. You were worthy of having your needs met as a child even though your parents may not have been able to give you what you needed.

This is not about blaming your parents; they were imperfect and likely did the best they could given the way they themselves were parented. *It is about becoming aware of how you felt and how you falsely interpreted certain experiences as a child.* Now, as an empowered adult woman, you can choose to believe the real truth about yourself.

You do this by becoming a loving parent to your inner little girl (as you learned in chapter two) and by *reprogramming your subconscious mind* so you can fully step into your power as a woman. If you don't know where a particular false or limiting belief came from, don't worry, you can still change and reprogram it.

*Your beliefs must be in alignment with what you want to create.* Believing you aren't worthy is just one kind of false belief, but a very common one. There are many others unique to each person that can prevent you from having what you want in love and life. For example, you may want to have a loving partner, but at the same time you may believe if you did have a partner, you wouldn't be able to take care of your health or you would sacrifice your freedom. These kinds of false beliefs need to be *reprogrammed with the exact opposite thoughts*—you can still take excellent care of your health and enjoy your freedom when you are in a loving relationship.

There are also circumstantial beliefs such as, "It's too late for me to attract love now because of my age, I'm too old." You have beliefs about yourself, men, women, relationships and life. It's really important to not only look at your conscious beliefs, but also to become aware of the subconscious beliefs which are actually running your life on auto pilot beneath the surface. Your subconscious is 90% of your mind, and your conscious mind is only 10%. The question is not whether a belief is true or not true. *The real question is which beliefs are you going to accept as true - for you?*

## EMPOWERED WOMAN PRACTICES FOR RELEASING FALSE BELIEFS AND REPROGRAMMING YOUR SUBCONSCIOUS MIND

*Remember, you must do the inner work to change what you think, feel and believe about yourself to change your outer experiences in love and life.*

**Note:** Programming your subconscious mind for what you want to create and manifest in your life will be discussed further with secret six in chapter six, because your subconscious programming greatly affects your ability to manifest what you want. Keep in mind that you have very likely had the same beliefs and feelings for many years (often since childhood) so it can take some time to reprogram the subconscious mind. It usually takes *at least* 30 days of practice and repetition for changes to last. Again, remember that changing how you *feel* is needed to make changes in your subconscious mind, just "thinking positive" is not enough.

**The seven steps below will help you to reprogram your subconscious mind with new beliefs, feelings and actions.**

**1.** Identify the false beliefs (and painful feelings) that are in conflict with what you want, by asking yourself why you think you can't or don't have what you want. The answers you receive are your false beliefs. Write each one down.

**2.** Although you don't have to know why or where the belief or feeling came from—*the point of power is always in the present*—it can be helpful. If possible, identify why the belief and feeling is there. You created a false belief because of some emotional pain in the past, often in your childhood. *The false belief is trying to cover up or explain that pain away.* Ask yourself what painful emotional experiences have you had in the past that are related to or similar to the challenges you are having now in your life? For example, if you want a loving, intimate relationship with a man, but you attract or are with emotionally unavailable men, did you perhaps have a father who was emotionally unavailable? If so, you likely formed the false belief that you must not have been worthy of your dad's emotional presence and care. You then grew up feeling that you aren't worthy of any man's emotional presence and care which is why you attract emotionally unavailable men. Even if you don't know why you have a belief, you can still proceed to step three.

**3.** *Connect with your heart and send love and compassion to yourself.* Remind yourself that you formed the belief as a defense mechanism to explain away and prevent yourself from feeling emotional pain. The love you feel and send to yourself now will raise your vibration, which then helps you release the false belief and connect with the deeper, spiritual truth.

**4.** *Keep connecting with your heart by placing one or two hands on it.* Your soul communicates the truth to you through your heart. Feel this connection and say, "I am willing to release this false belief and accept a new one." Then ask your heart or your Spiritual Source to tell you what the deeper truth is, what is the new belief that you are now free to choose and accept as your own. From this point forward, *what is going to be true for you?*

**5. *Next be willing to release the painful emotion that goes with the belief and practice feeling a new uplifting emotion.*** Write down the new belief and how you want to feel. Create a mantra or affirmation and program your subconscious mind with this new, true belief that is the *complete opposite* of the false belief. Repeat it with *real feeling* while *connecting with your heart and your body.* Looking at yourself in the mirror and smiling as you say the new belief can be very powerful. Feel as if you are breathing in the words and the energy of this new belief into your heart and into your body. Your body actually *is* your subconscious mind, but that's a topic for another book on the body-mind connection!

**6.** A belief is something you think and feel on a consistent basis, and beliefs and feelings are interconnected, as we discussed in chapter two. A belief is something that feels like truth to you, or something that you accept as truth. So, in addition to thinking new thoughts, take it deeper and ask yourself *what would it feel like to you if this new belief were true?* You must practice thinking the new thoughts, but also practice *feeling* how it would feel if you knew the new belief was true. This will shift your energy and change your whole state of being.

You will learn a powerful manifestation technique using music to help you program your desired feelings into your subconscious mind when we get to secret six in chapter six. In other words, consistently practicing feeling a certain way is needed to change subconscious beliefs. You need to change your self-concept *and* your emotional energy to align with what you want and practice a whole new way of being. Yes, you want to think new thoughts, but just as important, you need to be feeling the truth of the thought or belief by creating a new feeling reality within you. Why? **Because it's the feeling that carries the belief into your subconscious mind.**

**7. *In addition to practicing how it would feel to have the new belief, your actions and behaviors need to be those of your Empowered Woman Within.*** You are learning a whole *new way of being.* This is where many women have challenges because you have certain subconscious behavioral habits that you developed to help protect you and keep you safe, to meet a need for love or to help you to cope with something difficult in the past.

*When you start to change the habit or behavior pattern, very often a lot of fear will come up and cause you to slip back into old disempowering behaviors.* For example, you may have concluded that speaking up and saying no was not a good idea when you were a child, so you developed the habit of not speaking up about something that doesn't feel good to you. You carried this habit into your adulthood. Now as an adult woman, when you want to say no to someone, fear can come up to try to protect you, even though you know logically that it is perfectly safe for you to say no now to something that you don't want. We will explore the topic of safety and your subconscious mind a little deeper in chapter six.

Changing a false belief and reprogramming your subconscious mind very often involves facing a fear, and this why many women slip back into old habits. *But when you find the courage to face your fear and take action anyway, I assure you it will be very empowering and life changing.*

*To reprogram your subconscious mind, you need to change three things - your thoughts and beliefs, your feelings and emotions, and your actions and behaviors - to align with what you want.* The more you embody these changes, meaning the more you practice *being the new you,* the less you will have to consciously think about it. *Your energy will simply be different.* The changes you've made on the inside will start to be reflected in your outer world, *because you have experienced a change in your consciousness – and you have changed your energy with self-love.*

## THE MANY BENEFITS OF RELEASING FALSE BELIEFS

Releasing false beliefs and programming new true beliefs and uplifting emotions into your subconscious mind will positively affect your physical health, help you to lose weight, and reduce physical pain. As far as relationships, your subconscious mind will no longer be running your love life and causing you to choose, settle, and stay in relationships with partners that feel familiar but who are not good for you. You will stop trying to get from your partner, potential partners, or others what you didn't have as a child and what you need to be giving to yourself now. Your *Empowered Woman Within* will be in charge and will say no thank you to less than what and who you want and deserve. It is your own self-love that allows you to say no and to set healthy boundaries. *High self-worth, self-confidence, and self-love equal healthy boundaries and high standards.* Having healthy boundaries and standards is your empowered masculine energy supporting and protecting your empowered feminine energy.

## SELF-ESTEEM, CODEPENDENCY AND HEALTHY BOUNDARIES

**When you do not have healthy boundaries with others it is a sign that you are disconnected from your *Empowered Woman Within* and from your Spiritual Source.** When you feel this lack of connectedness, you will feel insecure and this will cause you to have difficulty forming healthy relationships. You will settle for less than you deserve or even tolerate mistreatment. For example, you may over give or do things that do not feel right or good to you because you fear losing someone's love.

Women often ask me why it's so hard for them to set boundaries. *Having difficulty setting healthy boundaries is a big sign that you need to increase your self-esteem and strengthen your sense of self.* You have to own yourself and know who you are. You have to know what you feel, think, and need. You have to have a healthy sense of self. ***Then you need to love yourself enough to communicate what you feel and need to others***.

This takes awareness and courage, because there's always a chance that someone will abandon or reject you, two of the most common fears women have in relationships. If that happens, it is giving you important information about your relationship with that person. *If the relationship only exists when you don't have healthy boundaries, then it is an unhealthy, codependent relationship.* Setting healthy boundaries will actually increase your level of self-esteem and self-confidence. Having a loving relationship with yourself is what gives you the power to attract or create truly healthy loving relationships with others.

Women who are codependent and in their disempowered feminine energy stay in relationships longer than what is best for them. They also may tend to think (on a subconscious level) that if they attract someone who needs them, then that person will never leave them. They often choose partners that they have to take care of in some way because they don't feel like they are good enough to be loved just for who they are.

## YOU CAN'T FIX OTHER PEOPLE

For example, if you are codependent, you may find yourself with someone who has some terrible problem, crisis, or challenging situation that you hope to help heal or fix. You then end up really being there for this person, staying by their side through the worst of it, in their time of great need. You may temporarily feel good about yourself for trying to help, but sooner or later you realize that you are in a one-way relationship where you are not getting any of your own needs met. Why is that? Because you believe you are just there to support and cater to a partner and their needs. When you're codependent and lacking in self-love and self-esteem, it's all about your partner or the other person and it is not a *mutually* loving relationship. This is why codependents tend to attract people who are self-absorbed and narcissistic.

*Narcissistic people are people that are very selfish and lack empathy for other people's feelings and needs*. Therefore, someone who is codependent is a perfect match for them, because the codependent, lacking in self-love and self-worth only cares about their partner's feelings and discounts and ignores their own. To someone who is narcissistic, a relationship is about having a partner cater to their needs, there is *no reciprocity* and caring about their partner's feelings and needs in return.

An important thing to understand is that sometimes the reason a codependent woman has this behavior pattern of being with someone who needs her help but who cannot or will not be there for her when she needs support, is because she is hoping that the man will *find value in her and therefore never leave her*. This is what I meant in the introductory chapter when I said that codependency is seeking from others what you are not giving to yourself, which is giving your power away.

An empowered woman has a healthy sense of self and really *values herself.* She is not seeking approval or trying to prove how worthy and valuable she is. If you don't value yourself, no matter how much someone else values you, it will never be enough. If you don't love yourself, no matter how much someone loves you, eventually their love will never be or feel like enough to you.

## THE POTENTIAL PROBLEM WITH EMPATHY

But isn't it a good thing to have empathy and want to help others? Yes, empathy and wanting to help is a wonderful thing, unless it's coming from a place of lack (not enough) or fear. *If you're helping someone because you don't feel good enough as you are, you're coming from a place of lack.* This is when a lot of women will over give, giving to others at the expense of their own health and well-being. This demonstrates a lack of self-love. This is why it's so important to be self-aware, to have an awareness of *why* you are doing what you are doing. What is *underneath* your helping and giving, are you really seeking someone's approval because you don't feel good enough, because you don't feel valuable and deep down you're hoping they will find value in you? Or are you giving from a full heart and a full place where you already value yourself and you're giving for the pure joy of giving to and helping someone in need?

**Over giving comes from a fear of rejection, abandonment, and/or loss.** Often when women fall in love, we start to feel vulnerable, and we become afraid that we are going to lose the love, so we subconsciously try to prevent that from happening by giving too much. If a man pulls away, we may fear we did something wrong and give even more. The giving is coming from a fear of losing love, of love leaving us. Or the giving might be coming from, I've got to prove that I'm valuable or earn someone's love. When you over give, you may also start to feel resentful, thinking, "I'm giving so much to them, so why aren't they giving to me?"

*Genuine giving comes from love.* If you're giving from love you won't feel resentful, and you won't have the expectation of getting love in return because you have healthy self-love. This doesn't mean you would ever stay in a one-way relationship, because when you love yourself, your relationship must be *mutually* loving. It means that there's a big difference between expecting to get love in return while not loving yourself -- and wanting to share love with another because you are filled with your own self-love. If you're giving to get something in return, it's giving from fear.

***Be honest with yourself and tune into the energetic motive that is underneath your giving.*** You may genuinely feel empathy for someone and want to help, but be sure the help and giving is not *also* coming from a place of fear and feelings of unworthiness, if it is, that is a problem pattern. To break this pattern, you need to practice self-love and be more giving to yourself. When you can do this, you will be more receptive to others giving to you. Remember, giving is masculine energy and receiving is feminine energy. If you tend to over give, practice allowing yourself to receive. Contrary to popular opinion, it is not "better to give than to receive." Receiving is just as important as giving, especially as a woman!

***Another potential problem with empathy is sometimes the more empathy you have, the more you might find yourself making excuses for someone's bad behavior.*** You may tolerate it because "he had a rough childhood." When you make excuses like this, you're not looking at how his behavior is negatively affecting you. At first when you change unhealthy relationship patterns, it may feel uncomfortable. It takes courage to be with your discomfort when you set boundaries and say no, and it may feel really uncomfortable to you if other people are unhappy with or disapproving of you. You will most likely need to remind yourself that it is not your responsibility to make other people happy, you are only responsible for your own happiness. In fact, this is one of the relationship spiritual truths you will learn about in chapter four.

***Please keep in mind that if you do not set a boundary when someone is being hurtful or behaving badly, you are enabling their unhealthy behavior.*** Many women get unconditional love and healthy boundaries confused. Love is something you feel for a person, but having boundaries involves taking action to care for and protect yourself. You can love someone unconditionally and still set a boundary. You can love someone and still decide to leave the relationship. In fact, you can set boundaries with love, which is what I teach.

## YOU ARE INNATELY WORTHY, VALUABLE AND LOVABLE

*When you're codependent and in your disempowered feminine energy, you are giving your sense of power and love to someone or something outside of you, while at the same time you have only conditional love for yourself.* It's "If he loves me, then I'm lovable. If he approves of me, then I'm good enough. If he commits to me and doesn't leave me, then I'm worthy and valuable."

But your *Empowered Woman Within* knows the deeper truth. If he doesn't love you, you're still lovable. If he doesn't approve of you, you're still good enough. If he doesn't want to commit to you and he leaves you and never wants to talk with you again, you're still worthy, valuable and lovable! *Your worth comes from the Divine, your worth is innate and within you.*

The bottom line is this: Strengthening your relationship with your Divine Source and cultivating an unconditionally loving relationship with yourself will help you to see, feel, and know this deeper truth. It will prevent you from giving your power away, it will help you to set healthy boundaries, and it will help you to become a more empowered woman in your relationships and in your life.

## HEALTHY BOUNDARIES

*As an empowered woman you have healthy boundaries and high standards, rather than needy expectations*. Many women get these two things confused. Let's start with boundaries and standards and then we'll discuss how they differ from needy expectations. Healthy boundaries will help you create higher quality relationships, more energy, and better health. When you have or are developing healthy boundaries and standards, you are basically moving from codependency, giving your power away, and a lack of self-love into increased self-love, high self-worth and self-empowerment. Remember, you need your own empowered masculine energy to support your empowered feminine energy. You set boundaries with your empowered masculine energy. Boundaries are about taking care of and protecting yourself. Your empowered masculine energy is meant to protect your feminine energy and your whole being, just the way you want a man or a partner to be protective of you.

Having boundaries is not about being rigid or selfish, and it's not about putting up walls or defenses. It's about getting really clear about what feels good and right to you, what is okay and not okay with you, what brings you more energy, and what depletes your energy, what is acceptable and not acceptable to you. It's having an awareness of how things feel to you, which is one reason why what you learned with secret two is so important. You need to be in tune with yourself and your feelings to be able to set healthy boundaries. *All of these empowered woman secrets are interconnected.*

Healthy boundaries really elevate you to your best self, your best health, your best relationships, and your best life. They provide support and protection for you and your feminine energy. They are also the limits that you set to avoid being hurt, abused, used, manipulated, or mistreated in any way.

*Boundaries vary from person to person.* I may have a boundary that you don't have. Something may be okay and acceptable to me, but not to you. Boundaries are about taking care of and protecting yourself and having your own back—whatever that means to you. *Healthy boundaries show you love, support, value, and respect yourself.*

There are personal relationship boundaries and professional relationship boundaries. For example, you might not allow yourself to over give (to give at the expense of your health or well-being) whether it's at work or in your intimate personal relationships. You can also have physical, emotional, sexual, spiritual, energetic, time, and financial boundaries.

*If you are setting a boundary and it is not being honored or respected by someone, that is a big red flag.* You cannot feel safe with someone who does not respect your boundaries. As an empowered woman, you will walk away from a relationship with someone that does not care about your feelings and that does not honor and respect your boundaries. Talk with them about it and then observe if it happens again. If you repeatedly express what feels good to you and what doesn't and there is no change in the other person's behavior, then it is up to you to respond in an empowered way and get yourself out of the situation or the relationship. In chapter five with secret number five, you will learn how to communicate in an empowered and loving way.

Here are a couple of examples where you may need to set a boundary. Perhaps you're dating someone and you realize that you're not getting enough sleep or not getting enough alone time. In this case, setting a healthy boundary would be talking with them and telling them that you need to get to bed earlier or that you need to have more time alone. Or maybe you need to set boundaries at work because your boss wants you to work overtime too often and it's affecting your ability to lead a balanced life. You then need to talk with your boss about ways to lighten your workload.

## THE IMPORTANCE OF HAVING HIGH STANDARDS

*In addition to boundaries, as an empowered woman you also want to have high standards, the basic necessary conditions that you are looking for in your relationships.* For example, one of your standards may be that any relationship that you have with someone must be mutually fulfilling and reciprocal, rather than being a one-way relationship where you're there for and giving to them, but they are very self-absorbed and not there for you.

Another example of a standard would be any partner or friend must be free of active addictions and have some self-control over their behavior. Or perhaps your relationship standard is that you need to have a partner who is responsible with money, or who will communicate when there is an issue instead of withdrawing and shutting down emotionally. The high standards that you hold will radiate out an energy and a vibration that people will feel, sometimes without your even having to verbalize your concerns. Boundaries usually must be verbalized; standards are the guidelines you require anyone you allow into your life to respect.

*You have to decide what your boundaries and standards will be. The healthier your boundaries and the higher your standards, the more your light will shine and the more you will radiate the energy of a self-confident, empowered, high-value woman.*

Sometimes men or other people will consciously or subconsciously test your boundaries to see how far they can go. If a man is testing your boundaries, he wants to know if you love and respect yourself or if you will sacrifice and betray yourself for him to do whatever he wants. When you don't want to do something because it doesn't feel right to you, will you do it anyway to please a man? Men and other people can sense this. That's how people know who they can take advantage of; it's an energy people feel. If you aren't confident and secure in yourself and you don't know your value and feel your worthiness on a deep level, you will have difficulty setting boundaries and your standards will be low. Someone who takes advantage of people will look for someone who isn't very confident because they won't have very good boundaries.

## THE DIFFERENCE BETWEEN BOUNDARIES AND NEEDY EXPECTATIONS

Let's look now at the difference between having healthy boundaries and having needy expectations. It's really important to understand the difference between the two.

### Healthy Boundaries

*When you know and honor your boundaries, you will radiate a highly attractive energy because boundaries equal self-love and self-respect.* They will be personal and unique to each woman. Many people mistakenly think you have to set boundaries in an aggressive or angry way, when in reality, *you can set healthy boundaries with love.* Many women have learned to people please because growing up it felt safer to not speak up. But if you don't speak up, you can become resentful or depressed because you are betraying yourself. Remember, the key to being an empowered woman is staying very much in tune with your feelings, needs, and desires. It's knowing your boundaries and standing up for yourself that elevates you to *empowered woman energy.*

*With boundaries you don't and can't make someone honor or respect your boundaries, you have to honor them for yourself.* For example, you may say to someone, "No thank you, I don't want to do that," or you can walk away from someone or something that doesn't feel good to you. You are taking action to honor your own boundaries. You cannot make someone else honor or respect your boundaries, you can communicate to someone what they are, but you set the boundaries for yourself. It's like saying, this is who I am, this is what I like, this is what I don't like, this is what is acceptable to me and not acceptable. This what I'm comfortable with and what I'm not comfortable with, this is okay, but this is not okay. *You can say no to something because you know what you want and deserve.*

## Needy Expectations

In contrast, needy expectations often come from the hurts and unmet needs of your inner little girl. Because of those unmet needs, often from childhood, you are now *demanding* that they be met by someone else. You may even feel that others owe you something. You have expectations when you don't have a strong sense of self, high self-esteem and self-respect and when you don't know how to meet your own needs and lovingly take care of yourself. You may even feel entitled.

*In other words, expectations are about trying to control someone else's behavior, which is completely different than having boundaries and standards, which are about you. When you set a particular boundary and you have a particular standard it's because that is what you need, and if you don't have what you need, then you take the action you need to take. You're not trying to control someone else.*

## THE DIFFERENCE BETWEEN BEING NEEDY AND HAVING NEEDS

*It's also very important to understand the difference between being needy and having healthy emotional needs, because neediness is connected to having expectations.* If you have unmet needs (from either your inner child or your adult self), that you aren't aware of, you may start demanding that someone else do for you what you're not doing for yourself. This is when you become needy, instead of having healthy emotional needs.

For example, when you abandon and reject yourself and then expect someone else to make you feel worthy and lovable, you are being needy. Neediness is very unattractive, and it repels healthy men and other people. Neediness is a common cause of relationship problems.

In contrast, we all have healthy emotional needs. For example, you are *not* being needy when you come to a partner or another person from your empowered woman self, needing emotional support as you cope with a difficult or painful experience. But when you come to a partner as your hurt inner little girl wanting him to *take responsibility for your feelings* you are being needy. You are also being needy when you are demanding more from a person than they are willing or able to give.

*Being needy is different than having needs*. Having needs is part of being human, but neediness and demanding or expecting someone to meet the needs they aren't even capable of meeting or that you're not taking responsibility for yourself is the opposite energy of a self-confident, empowered woman.


## HOW THE ENERGY OF EXPECTATIONS AND BOUNDARIES DIFFER

*When you have expectations there is a heavy, clingy, needy, demanding energy that goes with them.* An example would be expecting a man to introduce you to his family when he's not ready to do that yet. You're expecting him to be someone or somewhere that he is not. His reasons for doing something or not doing something may have nothing to do with you. What you want to do instead is to let go of your expectations and just observe people and their behavior. *Then you can set boundaries and act accordingly on your own behalf. With boundaries there is no needy, clingy or demanding energy, instead your energy communicates self-confidence and self-respect.*

Depending on the specific situation and relationship, you may want to talk with him, before making any decisions. But how you communicate and the energy underneath your words is very important. You'll learn about communication in chapter five.

The more you practice all of the empowered woman secrets in this book, the more clearly you will start to see people for who they really are and what they have to offer you. Then if you like what you see and are experiencing with them, you can continue the relationship.

If not, you can choose to end the relationship, or depending on the situation, you can still see them but open yourself up to dating other people as well. You can withdraw or stop putting so much energy into the relationship, thus creating a boundary. Keep in mind that you don't want to be giving and investing more energy in a relationship than the man is. Instead of over giving, you want to observe and match his level of emotional investment in the relationship and allow yourself to receive.

*The important thing to ask yourself when it comes to boundaries is, are you actually setting a healthy boundary or are you emotionally triggered and reacting with a needy expectation because of one of your own unmet needs from the past?*

*Of course, you will have healthy emotional needs in a relationship.* For example, you need to be with a partner with whom you feel safe and who you can trust, someone who will communicate with you when there is a problem. What I am saying is that you don't want to *demand* that someone meet your needs *or to try to change or control them*. You simply tell or ask them for what you need and observe what they do. Then take self-loving action accordingly on your own behalf.

## HEALTHY BOUNDARIES AND NEEDY EXPECTATIONS SUMMARY

*Boundaries are about having a deep sense of love and respect for yourself.* They are about you taking care of and protecting yourself. You have your own back. You know what you need and what you desire. There's a *self-confident, powerful energy* around you because you know that you can take whatever action you need to take for yourself. You respect yourself and you also respect other people because they have their own boundaries and standards. Setting healthy boundaries does not involve getting angry, emotionally triggered and reactive. It's not getting defensive or putting up walls. *You can set healthy boundaries with love, kindness, honesty, and assertiveness, and you respect and allow other people to have their boundaries also.*

*With expectations, you're placing a demand on someone else.* It is wonderful to express what you want, but placing expectations or demands on someone else is not healthy or helpful. If a man, person, job or situation is not offering you what you want and need, then you can back away or take whatever action you need to take on your own behalf. Expectations are really a form of *control and entitlement*, because you have the attitude and energy of, "I expect you to do this or that." In other words, expectations are an attempt to control someone else.

*With expectations there is a needy, controlling, or demanding energy, and it feels like you're placing a weight or burden on someone.* With boundaries, you have specific things that you need and want, and you have certain requirements and standards in your mind as you evaluate and observe the behavior of others. *Then you make choices and decisions for yourself based on what you see and observe.*

*Notice when you have expectations.* Depending on the relationship, you may be able to change an expectation into an agreement. *Expectations are always one-sided, but an agreement is between two people.* For example, if you work all day and your husband isn't working that particular day, you may have the expectation that he will make dinner. When you come home and dinner isn't made, you may feel angry or upset. Instead of demanding or expecting him to make dinner, you can instead talk with him and see if you can create *a mutual agreement that you both feel good about.* Perhaps he will agree to make dinner certain nights of the week etc. Then you can observe whether he keeps his agreements because that will tell you how committed and trustworthy he is.

## SECRET THREE SUMMARY

### How Being in Your Power In Chakra Three Helps You Create the Healthy Love and Life You Want and Deserve

**Health:** At the root of health challenges is often a lack of self-love and low self-worth. When you have high self-esteem and self-worth, you will take better care of your health. If you don't have healthy boundaries and you take on too much responsibility for other people's emotions or lives, it will drain your energy and undermine your health. Healthy boundaries actually protect your health. Reprogramming false beliefs will also help your overall health because you are being true to yourself and therefore will be living more in alignment with your heart and soul. Your body responds to and is affected by your mind and your emotions. Everything is interconnected.

**Love and relationships:** If you have low self-esteem, are needy, codependent, and/or have difficulty setting boundaries, you will likely attract people who also have low self-esteem and who are self-absorbed, narcissistic, or emotionally unavailable. Increasing your self-esteem, claiming your innate worthiness and having healthy boundaries and standards will elevate you to your best life and help you to attract healthy loving people into your life. Reparenting your inner child or reprogramming your false beliefs, increasing your self-confidence and changing your self-concept will help you release disempowering codependent relationship behavior patterns and replace them with healthy, self-loving, empowered woman habits. This then will allow you to attract or create the kind of healthy loving relationships and life that you truly want and deserve.

## CHAKRA THREE EMPOWERED WOMAN MANTRAS

*I am a powerful, self-confident woman.*
*I am worthy and good enough just as I am.*
*I have healthy boundaries and standards.*
*I feel worthy of receiving all that my heart desires.*

*I have high self-esteem.*
*I define my self-worth from within.*
*I am replacing false beliefs about myself with the truth.*
*I have a healthy sense of self.*
*I feel confident.*
*I feel worthy.*
*I believe that what I desire is possible.*
*I believe in myself.*
*I am a powerful woman.*
*I claim and own my innate worthiness now.*

When you have boundaries and standards you have your own back. You will then be able to fully open your heart to love. Let's explore this further as we move on to chapter four, secret four. It's time to discuss the power of your heart and your lovability. It's time to learn more about love—self-love, relationship love and Divine Love.

# EMPOWERED WOMAN
# SECRET FOUR

# CHAKRA FOUR

*Accepting Your Lovability, Connecting with Your Heart and the
Power of Love—Self-Love, Relationship Love and Divine Love*

# CHAPTER FOUR
# SECRET FOUR

The fourth empowered woman secret to creating the healthy love and life you want and deserve corresponds with your fourth energy center, your heart chakra, which is located in the center of your chest. It is associated with the colors green and pink. Pink represents self-love and green represents healing. Your heart chakra is about compassion, joy, kindness, forgiveness, gratitude, self-love, and love for others.

## CHAKRA FOUR – IN YOUR POWER

When you are in your power in your heart chakra you love and accept yourself unconditionally. You know and feel that you are lovable despite your imperfections. You know that love is your greatest power and that it is always available to you, both within you and around you. You choose to be loving, both when relating to yourself and when interacting with others. You connect with and listen to your heart.

Your heart is open to giving and receiving love from others as well as open to receiving Divine Love. You forgive yourself and others, you do not harbor resentment. You feel joyful, peaceful, and grateful. You are non-judgmental of yourself and others. You are also kind and compassionate with yourself and others, but you are not a doormat. You have boundaries and standards as we discussed with secret three, and are able to set those healthy boundaries with love.

## CHAKRA FOUR - NOT IN YOUR POWER

When you are not in your power in this center, you lack self-love and deep down you do not feel that you are lovable. Your heart may be closed or blocked because of old stuck anger, resentment, and an unwillingness to let go of past hurts. You may be detached from your emotions and unable to feel compassion for yourself or others. You may also repress painful emotions which can cause anxiety or depression. You may feel lonely, isolated, or rejected and have difficulty giving and receiving love in your relationships with others. You have difficulty connecting with the love inside your own heart, and you may be judgmental of yourself and others.

## THE POWER OF YOUR HEART

Let's begin by discussing the power of your heart. Your heart is the seat of your soul. *Your heart started beating when you were a little fetus in your mother's womb before your brain was even formed.* Isn't that amazing? It has its own intelligence. While it was once thought that the brain was the control center of our bodies, it has been scientifically proven that our brain actually receives many of the instructions that tell it what to do from our hearts. Your heart is always sending signals to your brain, and your brain responds to those messages.

Science has also discovered that we have over 40,000 specialized cells called sensory neurites in our hearts. These are brain-like cells that actually think, feel and remember independently from your brain. This means that you can ask your heart a question and it will give you its own answer. Your heart is a powerful center of intuitive intelligence; in other words, you can access your intuition through your heart which is where your soul communicates with you. Yes, you need your intellect and logic, but that alone is not enough. ***You need a connection to your heart to be happy and fulfilled in life.***

The best way to shift your focus from your thinking mind to your heart is to physically touch it in a way that's comfortable to you, such as placing one or both of your hands on it.

As I mentioned in chapter one, this will help release relaxing chemicals, reduce anxiety and help you feel more safe and secure.

If you repress or express your painful emotions in an unloving way to others, it creates a lack of harmony between your brain and your heart. To get the balance and harmony back between them, bring your awareness into your heart, then consciously bring up feelings of gratitude, appreciation, compassion and love. This will begin to shift your energy into what is referred to as heart coherence. Research by the HeartMath Institute has shown that this is one of the best ways to bring your brain and your whole nervous system into a more calm, coherent (harmonious), balanced and relaxed state.

*Love is the most powerful energy in the universe. Although love can feel like an emotion, it's actually much more. Love is an electromagnetic field, a loving intelligence that permeates all of life.* The heart's electromagnetic field is tremendously powerful and intelligent. This loving intelligence and electromagnetic field of love emanates from your heart throughout your whole body and into the energy field around your body, which is called your aura. Your heart radiates loving energy out to others as well. To become a more empowered woman, you must connect with and listen to your heart. *How often do you connect with your heart?*

The heart is a feeling organ, whereas the brain is a thinking organ; the brain is about thought and logic while the heart is about love and emotion. The heart emits an electromagnetic field 40-60 times greater than that of the brain. Consciously tune in and connect with your heart on a daily basis. Bring your attention to your heart by placing a hand on it, asking a question and then really tune in and listen to what your heart tells you.

## BENEFITS OF CONNECTING WITH YOUR HEART

Scientific studies have shown that when you focus on your heart, the magnetic field around your body grows larger. Magnetic equals attractive, so connecting with your heart helps you to manifest whatever you want in your life, especially when it comes to love and loving relationships! In addition, as I discussed in chapter one, the energy of trust is found inside your heart, so it helps you release anxiety and stress.

A strong connection to your heart is what allows you to have healthy, intimate relationships and a meaningful, fulfilling life. Tuning into your heart will give you clarity about what you truly want in your life and about any situation or relationship that you are in. You will not find out what your deepest desires are in your head; you can only find them in your heart!

Your heart is also a powerful intuitive center, therefore it can provide you with the guidance you need if you simply tune in, ask for, and then listen to your heart's answer. As you connect with your heart, you will be able to communicate with love and express your feelings authentically with open-hearted vulnerability, instead of communicating with neediness, demands, and unhealthy emotional attachment. You will be more able to respond with love instead of reacting from fear. We'll discuss empowered loving communication in chapter five with secret five.

When you are in your heart you are receptive. Receptivity is your empowered feminine energy. You are receptive when you have a non-judgmental mind. With an open heart, rather than being judgmental of others or yourself, you have true compassion.

*The next time you're in a conflict or a tense situation with someone, begin focusing on your heart.* The other person doesn't have to know what you are doing. As you focus on your heart, you might stop talking and begin to deeply listen. You may be surprised at how this subtle practice can shift the energy in a situation in a loving direction when conflict arises. The biggest challenge is remembering to do it, because we are trained to stay focused in our heads, thinking we need to resolve conflict with our minds. The mind alone cannot resolve a conflict with a loved one. Remember to focus on your heart when you are in a tense situation and notice what happens.

*Your heart speaks to you all the time; the question is, are you listening?* Ask your heart how it feels about certain people, places, and things. When I coach people who are confused and in their heads, I sometimes ask them to close their eyes, focus on their hearts, and then ask for the answer to their question. The clear and true guidance that they receive from their heart rather than trying to figure everything out with their head often amazes them. Ask your heart what it wants often, what brings you joy in life, and what lights you up. Music and dance will do that for me. I find that when I dance, I feel joy in my heart and then I start to feel more love for myself, others, and for life itself.

Go within and ask yourself what your heart is really longing for right now. Believe and tell yourself that what you want is absolutely possible. For most women their sense of possibility in life is based on either their past experiences or their present circumstances. The secret of the empowered woman is that you are defining your identity based on the future that you want. You're in the process of creating that future and you're open to infinite possibilities and support from the universe! You will learn more about this in chapter six. *For now, know that following your heart's deepest desires is an aspect of self-love.*

## SELF-LOVE

This whole book is really about self-love. We discussed loving your body in chapter one, loving yourself emotionally in chapter two and working with your mind and your beliefs especially related to your sense of worthiness in chapter three. We also discussed having healthy boundaries and high standards, important aspects of self-love, in chapter three.

Your relationship with yourself is the foundation for your relationships with other people, for people will often love you the way you love yourself. Self-love is caring about your own health and well-being, on all levels—physically, emotionally, mentally and spiritually. It is listening to your heart's yearnings and acting upon your heart's desires. Self-love is an ongoing practice, something that you must commit to daily. It is having an ongoing, life-affirming, loving relationship with yourself. Even though there are actions you can take to cultivate self-love, the experience and *feeling* of self-love is not in your mind, it's something you *feel in your heart*. *Our mind doesn't really understand love the way our heart does.*

## THE ENERGY BEHIND SELF-LOVE IS KEY

When discussing self-love it's important to understand that loving yourself won't be very healing or life changing if the *energy* underneath your self-love feels like, "No one loves me, therefore I just need to love myself." Or, "I feel really unloved by others, so I guess I just need to love myself." Or, "I always get hurt in love so I better just love myself." If you are walking around feeling unloved and hurt most of the time and perhaps even feeling sorry for yourself, your energy will be communicating "unloved and hurt by others," and you need to change that kind of energy and pattern to attract healthy, true love in your life! How you feel about yourself is so important. The energy behind your self-love needs to be and feel more like, "I love myself because I'm an amazing woman. I love myself because I have so many wonderful qualities. I love who I am. I am so lovable and I love sharing my love with others!" Can you feel the difference?

## SELF-LOVE AND CODEPENDENCY

When I say that your relationship with yourself is the foundation for your relationships with others, I am not saying that you must love yourself perfectly before you get into a relationship. Self-love is an ongoing practice and journey and being in a relationship can actually help you to see the ways in which you are not loving yourself and the ways that you need to learn to love yourself. ***One of the most common patterns that comes up in relationships is codependency.***

We've discussed disempowered feminine energy and codependency a few times in earlier chapters. Here I want to emphasize and further define how it relates to self-love. Codependency is really a lack of self-love and self-care which causes you to lose your center, disconnect from your own feelings and needs, and give your power away in your relationships. **It's hyper-focusing on giving your love and care freely and abundantly to others while undervaluing, dismissing or not feeling worthy of that same love and care from others in return.** In contrast, when you're connected to your *Empowered Woman Within*, you love yourself and have *mutually* loving relationships with others.

## FALSE MESSAGES ABOUT SELF-LOVE

We get so many false messages from our society about self-love. One false message is that if you love yourself, it means that you are conceited, arrogant, or narcissistic. This is completely false! You cannot love yourself too much, and if someone is conceited, arrogant, or narcissistic it means that they actually have low self-esteem and suffer from a tremendous lack of self-love.

The other common, false message about self-love is that it is selfish. Again, this is totally false. To be selfish means that you don't care about other people's feelings, needs, or desires. A selfish person is very often not aware of other people's needs or feelings because they are so self-absorbed. They lack empathy. Selfishness is *not caring* about how your behavior may affect someone else. With self-love, you love yourself and you also care about other people's feelings and needs and how your behavior may affect them. At the same time you can still take care of yourself and choose to do or not do something that someone wants you to do when it does not feel right or good for you.

***Self-love is being true to yourself.*** When you are true to yourself, you can't go wrong. Loving yourself and being true to yourself is always going to be for the highest and best good for everyone else involved, even if other people don't realize it at the time and are not happy with what you decide is best for you. As an empowered woman who loves herself, you hold the belief that any choice you make to take care of and love yourself blesses not only you but also blesses other people as well. ***When you are true to yourself, it will ultimately be for the highest good for everyone involved.***

***Self-love takes courage and commitment.*** When you love yourself, you don't abandon yourself with addictions, self-criticism, or disempowering codependent relationship behaviors. You have compassion for yourself and you let go of perfectionism. You accept all parts of yourself. You feel lovable just the way you are, despite your imperfections.

Self-love is an ongoing practice and it includes loving yourself emotionally - remember the three question emotional mastery practice from chapter two, where you ask yourself:

What are you feeling?

What are you needing?

What loving action can you take to meet this need?

*Attending to your emotional needs is an important aspect of self-love.*

As you go through your day, start to notice when you are being loving or unloving to yourself. When you catch yourself being unloving, ask yourself what would be more loving? Underneath health, life, or relationship challenges, there is almost always a lack of self-love. Remember, loving yourself is healing yourself.

## EMPOWERED WOMAN PRACTICE – A LOVE LETTER TO YOURSELF

Write a beautiful love letter to yourself. Include things that you love and appreciate about yourself. Write about your unique qualities, your gifts, and talents. Write about your goodness, your worthiness, your lovability, how courageous you are, and how many challenges you have overcome. Write about the difference you have made in other people's lives. Shower yourself with compliments, praise, validation, appreciation, compassion, and love. Keep a copy of this letter nearby or even carry it with you. Read it when you need to remind yourself what an amazing and wonderful woman you are. Read it to help you to *feel* really good about yourself! Remember, how you *feel* about yourself is so important in relationships and in every aspect of your life.

## SELF-LOVE AND SELF-ACCEPTANCE

Part of self-love is knowing and loving yourself in all of your magnificence. But the other aspect of self-love is loving and accepting yourself when you're in emotional pain, experiencing fear, loneliness, sadness and any other uncomfortable emotion. It's accepting your imperfections and really being there for yourself through the difficult times, just as you would want another person to be there with you. This deep self-love and acceptance of your whole self will help keep your heart open to love in all forms.

## SELF-COMPASSION AND SELF-FORGIVENESS

Another aspect of loving yourself is having compassion for yourself. When you are compassionate, your heart is open to yourself. Rather than criticizing and judging yourself, practice being present to yourself when you are in pain just as you are understanding and caring with others who are suffering.

Be understanding and caring and feel empathy for yourself in difficult situations. This will feel very comforting, especially if you are experiencing anxiety. In fact, you may find that anxiety and stress greatly diminish when you feel and express not only love, but also compassion for yourself. Again, loving yourself is very healing to yourself on all levels, and compassion is part of love. Self-forgiveness is another part of self-love. Forgive yourself for being human, for making mistakes, for not being perfect, for having challenges, and for hurting or causing someone else pain. We will discuss forgiveness at the end of this chapter.

## CONNECT WITH YOUR HEART AND SHIFT YOUR ENERGY WITH LOVE

You can shift your energy with love in all of your chakras. With chakra one, when you connect with your heart, you feel the energy of trust, which helps you to relax, feel safe, and love your body. With chakra two when you connect with your heart, you hold a loving space for all of your emotions. With chakra three you can connect with your heart and Divine Love to help you to rewire false beliefs. And in chakra four, you practice self-love, self-compassion, and opening your heart to giving and receiving love with others. You can also open your heart to receive Divine Love.

As we discussed earlier, many women at times feel unlovable, unworthy or not good enough. To increase your level and depth of self-love it can be very helpful to have some kind of spiritual practice, such as prayer or meditation, which we will discuss in chapter seven. Remember, you want to connect with that wise, empowered woman inside you on a consistent basis, for this is the part of you that knows your deeper truth. Your *Empowered Woman Within* knows that you are lovable and worthy of all that your heart desires. When you connect with your heart and your Spiritual Source, it will help you to release those false beliefs and align with the truth as we discussed with secret three. The reason your heart knows the truth is because *it is the bridge between your human self and your divine self.* You connect with your *Empowered Woman Within* and your soul by connecting with your heart, by connecting to love, and by opening your heart to receive Divine Love.

## OPENING YOUR HEART TO RECEIVE DIVINE LOVE

You give and receive love with other people through your heart. But as an empowered woman you know that other people are not your ultimate source of love. Your ultimate source of love is your Spiritual Source or Divine Love. You came from love and at your deepest essence, you are love because you are made of this loving intelligence and energy.

*This means that you have the ability to feel love in any given moment; you don't have to be with a certain person to be able to feel love's energy because love is within you.* Once you connect with it through your heart, you can then bring that love into your body to heal or change your physical condition and health with love. You can bring love to your own emotions and heal your hurts or fears. You can connect with this love to release false beliefs and remind yourself of the deeper truth. As you bring this love into your own heart, you will feel more love for yourself and be able to give and receive an abundance of love with others.

I'm not saying that all you need is Divine Love and self-love, because as human beings we are wired for and need loving relationships and connection with others. But if you want to have healthy, happy relationships you want to be *sharing* your love with others, giving and receiving love, rather than trying to *get* the love from them that you have not been giving to and feeling within yourself.

Just as we discussed earlier with self-love, the energy underneath your connecting with Divine Love is also very important. You don't want your energy to feel like, "No one loves me, I feel so unloved, so I'll just connect with Divine Love, at least my Spiritual Source loves me." Rather you want your feelings and energy to be and feel more like, "I love connecting with my heart and feeling my connection to Divine Love. It feels so good to connect with all of the love that is within me and around me!" Can you feel the difference?

## EMPOWERED WOMAN PRACTICE – RECEIVING DIVINE LOVE

The next time you are seated doing some form of prayer or meditation or perhaps sitting outside in nature, lean back slightly and imagine the beautiful light of Divine Love flowing down from above through your head and neck and filling your heart. Imagine or have the intention of opening your heart to receive it. As it fills your heart, imagine it radiating out through your whole body. The more you practice receiving this Divine Love and loving yourself, the more you will feel like you are *giving to others from a full place* and that you want to *share* your love as I mentioned earlier, rather trying to *get* the love that you haven't been giving to yourself. You will also be more open to *receiving* love from others as well.

***Imagine and feel that your heart is overflowing with love. As an empowered woman, you know that when you connect with the love inside your heart, there is no lack of love.*** You feel a sense of wholeness and completeness within yourself, which doesn't mean that you don't want to have a relationship and share your love with a partner. What it means is that you are not lacking love. Why? Because when you connect with and feel the love that is always there within your heart, you can feel that love both for yourself and others at any time.

When most women want a loving relationship with a partner, they think and feel, "I'm single, and I'm looking for love," and they are in the energy of "I'm trying to find love and get love from out there." Or they are trying to *get* more love from their partner. Instead, try affirming silently or out loud, "I am whole and complete, and *I am open and receptive to love*. My heart is overflowing with love and I'm looking so forward to sharing this love with my ideal partner." Notice the difference in your energy between the two kinds of statements and feelings. As an empowered woman you know that love is already within you and that you don't have to search for it externally. I'm not suggesting that you don't take any action in the outer world toward what you want. I'm saying that you want to notice what the energy is and what the feelings are underneath your actions. Is it the energy of fear and neediness or is the energy of love, curiosity, exploration and fun? When your heart is filled with Divine Love and self-love you know that you are lovable exactly the way you are and that you are worthy of receiving love. Then it won't be long until your outer world reflects this and you become a magnet for more and more love. I've had clients meet their soulmates in the most unlikely places, and quite often when they weren't "looking" and when they least expected it!

## ACCEPTING AND CLAIMING YOUR LOVABILITY

Learning to love yourself is truly the greatest love of all. One of the biggest reasons many women don't have the loving relationship they want is that deep down they don't feel lovable. The truth is that you were born lovable. You are lovable now, and you will always be lovable. Repeat to yourself daily. "I am lovable. I am lovable exactly as I am. I always have been and always will be lovable. I am deeply lovable." *In other words, one of the most important prerequisites you need to have a deep, loving relationship with another is the belief that you are lovable.*

*It is your birthright to have loving relationships and to be surrounded by loving people and relationships that support and nurture you, whether it's your family, your friends or an intimate partner.* You deserve unconditionally loving, kind, supportive people in your life, right now no matter what you have achieved or not achieved in your life, and despite your imperfections. Nothing has to be added and nothing needs to be taken away to make you more lovable. You are lovable just the way you are. You're not your past, you're not any of the relationships you've been in that were hurtful. If someone loved you but then left you, they didn't take everything they loved about you. Those things are still with you, and you are still lovable.

*You deserve to be unconditionally loved. What conditions are you placing on your lovability?* You deserve to have loving people supporting you in your life both in the happiest of times and during the most difficult and unhappy times. Love is not to be earned, chased, bought, or worked for; it is to be given and received. You don't have to prove that you deserve love, you just have to know that you are worthy of love and that you are lovable.

**Your imperfections actually make you deeply lovable, unique, and endearing**. Love all of you, your strengths and vulnerabilities, your gifts and learning opportunities, your amazing qualities and the things you want to improve or change. True unconditional self-love is loving your whole, complete self. It's loving all parts of you.

As you learn to love yourself you will not accept a level of love from another person that is lower than the level of love that you have for yourself. Likewise, if you don't feel lovable, you will have a hard time accepting and receiving a level of love that is higher than the level of love you have for yourself, in fact, you might even sabotage love or unknowingly push it away.

Start saying out loud to yourself the things that you would love to hear a partner or another loved one say to you such as, "You are the best thing that has ever happened to me. I just love you so much; you mean so much to me; you're so important to me, etc." Let your words nourish your heart and soul and fill you with the truth that you are lovable. You don't need to search for love because at your deepest essence, you are love. As you accept, claim and verbalize to yourself that you are lovable, you allow others to recognize that you are lovable also, and this will help you to attract and maintain love.

## ATTRACTING OR INCREASING LOVE WITH A PARTNER

*What makes you really attractive and magnetic is the energy of love that radiates from your heart.* It's not about what you look like or what you say. It's the love energy you're holding within yourself, your vibration. This energy influences *how* you say and do things. Ultimately, it's being in your heart that will bring you what you want. When you're open and receptive to the world, people will feel it. Within love is the energy of trust and it's this empowered feminine energy that makes you open, receptive, and approachable. This is the complete opposite of having walls up around your heart and closing off your energy because of fear.

*The only hindrance to being in the energy of love is fear.* As an empowered woman you are open, receptive and inviting. You are more approachable and attractive when you are happy and have an open heart and when you are authentic, confident, and warm. This warmth and radiance is like a light around you. Become more aware of your energy, is radiating love or fear? Are you in your heart? When you feel grateful and appreciative, you are in your heart. When you feel compassion and forgiveness, you are in your heart. When you are kind, you are in your heart.

*In addition, become aware of your emotional patterns in relationships*. Attracting a loving partner or improving your relationship with your partner is not just about loving yourself, it often requires changing the painful feeling patterns and energy that you've been carrying about yourself, men, women, or relationships. For example, it's going to be hard to attract a loving man if you have negative feelings and beliefs about men in general, or if you have a fear of getting hurt in a relationship. In addition to practicing self-love, these feeling patterns (and beliefs) need to be changed and reprogrammed as we discussed with secret three and will discuss further with secret six when you learn more specifically about manifesting your heart's desires.

To be loving to yourself and to others requires commitment. In a relationship, it's easy to be loving when everything is wonderful, but when you're going through a hard time or your fears come up and you get emotionally triggered, then committing to love can be a more challenging.

## EMOTIONAL TRIGGERS AND PATTERNS IN RELATIONSHIPS

Have you ever noticed that sometimes no matter how much good relationship advice you receive, you find yourself in the same kind of unfulfilling relationship again and again? That is because we have subconscious relationship patterns and programming that can cause us to be attracted to men that aren't good for us. *When you change these patterns, you will be changing your energy, and you will be attracted to a different kind of man.*

If you are in a relationship and wondering if you should stay or go, when you work on yourself and change your own emotional triggers and patterns, you will get the clarity and guidance you need about what to do.

*Change can happen in many different ways in relationships*. Sometimes one person's emotional triggers can trigger the other person and neither of them is aware of what's happening. This happens when people have what are referred to as different "love attachment styles." A classic example of this is when the anxious love attachment style person is in a relationship with the avoidant love attachment style person. One of the partners (the anxious style) has a fear of abandonment and wants more closeness and connection while the other (the avoidant style) has a fear of engulfment and wants more space. When both people become consciously aware of what's happening and are willing to work on the issues, wonderful changes can happen in the relationship. If they are unaware of the dynamics, it can be very challenging and painful.

*Positive changes can also happen in a relationship when just you become aware of your own emotional triggers and relationship patterns, and you start changing yourself and how you interact with the other person.* The key to transforming unhealthy or unfulfilling relationship patterns is making the changes within yourself, then those positive changes will either be reflected in your outer relationships or you will know that it's time for you to move on from a relationship. Ask yourself with love and compassion (not criticism or blame) why you might have attracted a certain kind of man. When you have the answer to that question and change the subconscious pattern, you'll be attracted to a different kind of man, someone who will be a much better match for the new you and your new way of being.

Do your best to be curious and compassionate with both yourself and other people. We all have our emotional triggers and relationship patterns. We are all doing the best we can with our current level of consciousness. Awareness is the first step to making any change in yourself and in your relationships. Be self-reflective and know that there are deeper reasons why you have certain relationship patterns and why you are now or have been in relationships with certain people in the past.

## RELATIONSHIP SPIRITUAL TRUTHS

*A good question to ask yourself is: "Why do I want to be in a relationship; what is the deeper reason?"* I personally believe that we are here on this planet to evolve and grow and to learn about love. I can't think of a better school for learning about love than to be in an intimate relationship with a partner. We learn about love in all of our relationships, especially with our family. Whatever you learned in your family will often get recreated in your adult life. In other words, you attract similar experiences that bring up the feelings from your childhood in your adult intimate relationships. You then not only have the opportunity to change whatever is going on in the current relationship, but also to understand and heal whatever happened to you in the past. Understanding the following four spiritual relationship truths will help you to grow, heal, and learn about love and the deeper purpose for being in a relationship. The spiritual text, *A Course in Miracles* says that relationships are our "spiritual assignments."

**The first relationship spiritual truth is—It is not your responsibility to make another person happy.** Believing it's your job to make other people happy is a very common, false, conscious or subconscious belief that many women have. Of course, you want the best for those that you love, but there is a big difference between loving someone and taking responsibility for their happiness.

*The truth is that you can only create your own happiness. You can care for others and love them deeply, but their happiness is up to them and out of your control.* Keep in mind that when you believe that you are responsible for someone else's happiness, you will also subconsciously believe that they are responsible for your happiness. You will want them to take responsibility for your feelings, but as we discussed in chapter two, your emotions are yours to own and master. As an empowered woman you take full responsibility for your own emotional health and well-being and your happiness. You do not believe that someone else has more power over your life than you do, for that is giving your power away. The peace, love and happiness you want and the changes you want to make in your life come from the inside out. You are the key, and you are the power. Your power is always within.

**The second relationship spiritual truth is that other people are our mirrors.** What this means is that everything that comes up in a relationship is an opportunity for you to look inside yourself. This is not about blaming yourself. It is becoming aware of what is being mirrored back to you in your relationship so that you can heal and grow. If you keep attracting men who are not really there for you and are not emotionally present, ask yourself, "Am I really there for myself? Am I emotionally present to myself?" If you're not emotionally available to yourself and you've been abandoning yourself when you have painful emotions, then very often you will attract a man who does not acknowledge your emotions and who is not emotionally there for you. He will often mirror back to you your own relationship with yourself, not always, but often. Relationships become hard when you seek from others what you are not giving to yourself.

Whenever you have relationship challenges and you get emotionally triggered, go within and connect with your feelings, needs, and desires as we talked about in chapter two. Connect with your heart and soul, rather than trying to fix or change the other person. Whatever happens in your relationship, ask yourself, "What is this bringing up in me right now? What is going on inside of me?"

**The third relationship spiritual truth is that you must love yourself the way you want to be loved by others.** As an empowered woman you want to create within you what is referred to as the "sacred marriage within." This is an internal, harmonious relationship between your empowered feminine energy and your empowered masculine energy. For example, when you have healthy boundaries (your empowered masculine energy) this allows you to open your heart and be in your empowered feminine energy. If you want a man to protect you, then you start protecting yourself. If you want a man to care about your feelings, you need to care about your own feelings. Love yourself the way you want to be loved. When your empowered masculine energy lovingly supports your empowered feminine energy, this harmonious dynamic will then be reflected in the relationships you have with other people, your partner or potential partners.

**The fourth relationship spiritual truth is that you cannot change another person, you can only change yourself.** The interesting thing is that when you change yourself, it can sometimes change your relationship. Don't go into a relationship thinking you can change someone and if you are already in a relationship, don't try to change your partner. *When you try to change someone else, you are in the energy of fear and control.* No one likes to feel like you are trying to change or control them because that is the opposite of love and acceptance. If you want to make changes in a relationship, rather than focusing on the other person, focus on yourself and changing how you're responding to the other person. Change your perception of what's going on. It's amazing that often when you let go of thinking your happiness depends on someone else changing, it will often create positive changes in the relationship. Try to look at your relationship with a partner or other significant people in your life as a vehicle for your own emotional and spiritual growth.

*When you want to change anything about someone or something about your life, it is usually because you want to feel a certain way.* For example, you think that if your partner would just do this or that, then you would be happy. But the truth is you can feel however you want to feel right now and as we just discussed with relationship spiritual truth number one, you are responsible for your own happiness. Remember your feelings are energy and you can actually shift your emotional state anytime you wish. Allow yourself to feel the painful emotions, but then choose to cultivate and feel uplifting emotions such as gratitude and appreciation. You can use whatever is happening in your relationships to learn, heal, or grow.

I'm not saying it's wrong to want your partner to treat or love you in a certain way, or that it's not okay to ask for what you want or need. That is perfectly okay and healthy. What I'm saying is that if you're not already giving yourself what you need and want first, eventually whatever amount of love someone else gives you will never feel like enough. If your heart truly desires a healthy, loving relationship, you must learn how to love yourself.

Connect with your heart and practice treating yourself how you would treat the people you love the most in your life. See your relationships and the challenges that come up with others as opportunities for you to learn more about how to love yourself and others unconditionally. As you focus on changing yourself, observe what happens in the relationship, then you will get the clarity you need about any action you need to take.

Connecting with your heart and soul is loving yourself and being intimate with yourself. This allows you to have a truly healthy intimate relationship with another person. Whether you are already in a relationship or you are wanting to be in one, your heart is always where the power is. ***Being in your heart is being in your power as a woman.***

The more you connect with your heart and stay in your *Empowered Woman Within* energy, the healthier and more fulfilling your relationship will become if the two of you are meant to be together. And if you realize that is it time to part ways, you will be able to do it with love, compassion, and forgiveness for both you and your partner. Forgiveness is something an empowered woman practices on a regular basis and it is the final topic for this chapter on the heart chakra.

## FORGIVENESS -THE ULTIMATE SPIRITUAL PRACTICE IN RELATIONSHIPS

We can't discuss the heart chakra and love without talking about forgiveness. Unconditionally loving yourself and others involves forgiveness and letting go of anger. As I said earlier, one of the main things that blocks your heart chakra and keeps you out of your power is old stuck anger and resentment. Unconditionally loving someone doesn't mean that you stay in a relationship if it is not best for you. You can unconditionally love someone and end or leave a relationship.

There are many misconceptions about forgiveness. Forgiveness is not something you do with your head, it is something you do with your heart. We all make mistakes and we all have past wounds that trigger us emotionally and cause us to hurt others, especially in our most intimate relationships. You can decide with your mind that you want to forgive, and that is a great first step, but the forgiveness itself happens in your heart, and it is a process. How long the process of forgiveness takes will vary depending on the nature of the hurt and many other factors. Sometimes you may think that you have forgiven someone, but then when you encounter the person again, it brings up more feelings for you.

Forgiveness is not really about the other person; it's about you. It's about freeing yourself from a painful emotional charge and connection that you have to a person who hurt you. Forgiveness does not mean that you are condoning someone's behavior (or your own behavior when you practice self-forgiveness) or that their behavior was okay. It doesn't mean that if you forgive someone that you're going to see them, talk with them, or have a relationship with them. You can forgive someone and still know that it is best for you is to not have contact with this person, especially if their hurtful behavior is unlikely to change. Forgiveness happens in your heart. You will know you have forgiven someone when you feel free from the emotional pain and anger that has been bonding you to this person.

I have had students and clients ask me if forgiveness means forgetting about the hurtful thing someone did. Forgiveness is not forgetting. You can remember something that was painful in the past, but no longer feel the pain in the present. When you remember, you honor what you learned from the situation, the wisdom and growth you gained from that experience. Your goal is to turn pain into wisdom and growth. Forgiveness means that you don't have an emotional charge about it anymore; the anger is gone and does not come up when you think about it.

I believe that there are four parts to forgiveness whether you are forgiving yourself or another person. First, you need to allow yourself to feel the anger because if you deny your anger, you will never get to forgiveness. Secondly you need to allow yourself to feel all of the more vulnerable feelings that are usually beneath your anger—the hurt, sadness, grief, the loss of trust, and feelings of betrayal. You need to allow yourself time to feel all of those feelings, no matter how uncomfortable.

*The third part of forgiveness is understanding that when people hurt others it is coming from their own fear, pain, or unconsciousness.* If we are mentally well and healthy, we usually don't want to hurt someone. As you begin to understand this, you might even feel some compassion for the other person and their pain. This is definitely not saying that you approve of what they did, or that you don't take loving action on your own behalf.

*Everything that happens to you, including your most painful experiences make you the person that you are right now, so the fourth part of forgiveness is about finding meaning in the pain you experienced.* This is done by transforming your pain into psychological or spiritual growth. Perhaps you have become more compassionate with others because of what happened. While you can't change another person or what happened, you can always ask yourself what you learned and how you grew through the experience. This is how you can become the alchemist and spin straw into gold. The meaning you find in your painful experience will be unique and personal to you. The question you want to ask yourself is what meaning am I going to give it? *Keep in mind that you don't need to understand why something happened in order to find the meaning in it and that it may take several months or even years to discover.*

A student in one of my classes once asked me if I believed that some things are unforgivable. I replied that I've seen some people hold onto resentment and grudges for years for the smallest things and then there are people who have forgiven the worst atrocities that you can imagine. I believe we all have varying degrees of ability to forgive anything and everything. Remember you're not condoning what someone did, and you're not forgetting about it. You're learning from it and transforming the pain into wisdom and growth.

You truly know that you've forgiven someone when you're actually able to feel some gratitude for the painful experience that you had with them. The relationship I mentioned in the introduction was one of my greatest teachers, and I feel grateful for it. Even though the hurt I experienced with this man that I loved very much was deep, at the same time, it really helped me to grow because it was the catalyst for me to heal my deepest wounds.

You can develop or strengthen certain qualities such as compassion, gratitude, and appreciation through painful experiences. This is not to say that you're going to say thank you to someone for hurting you, but you can feel gratitude for what you learned from the situation, and this will help you let go and forgive. Remember relationships are our "spiritual assignments."

One of the best things I have read on forgiveness comes from Nelson Mandela who was imprisoned in South Africa for over 25 years. The amazing thing was that after he got out prison, he said that he did not feel any anger, resentment, or bitterness. Many people could not understand how that could be possible, and so they asked him how he could not be angry after such a horrible experience. Nelson Mandela would answer by saying that when the door opened and he walked out of prison, he knew that if he did not leave all of his anger, hatred, and bitterness behind, he would still be in prison. ***Forgiveness is not about the other person. It is about freeing yourself.***

There is one more thing that I want to say about forgiveness that is related to your power. If someone does something that is hurtful to you and you hold onto that anger until it turns into resentment, you are building walls around your heart. That resentment will diminish your ability to give and receive love. Forgiveness is healing because it allows you to keep your heart open to giving and receiving love. If you remain angry, you are giving your power away because it is saying to the other person, "I'm going to give you and what you did the power to diminish my ability to give and receive love. I'm giving you and what you did the power to keep my heart closed."

But when you practice forgiveness, you are taking your power back and saying, "Yes, what you did was painful to me. It was definitely not okay, and I'm going to allow myself to feel all of my painful feelings about it. And I'm also not going to let this painful experience close down my heart, I'm not going to become bitter. I'm not going to give you or what you did the power to diminish my ability to give and receive love. I'm going to let go. I'm going to learn and grow from it. I'm going to allow this experience to break my heart *open* and love even deeper the next time because of it, rather than close down my heart with bitterness and resentment."

As an empowered woman, you know that you cannot control everything that happens to you, but you can choose how you are going to respond to what happens, and that is truly your greatest power. We all make mistakes. We are all here to learn about love and forgiveness. You cannot be an empowered woman if you are stuck in the past. As an empowered woman you transform your pain into gold. *In other words, you transform it into wisdom and growth, and a deeper ability to give and receive love.*

## SOUL LEVEL HEALING AND COMMUNICATION

One of the most painful things that can happen in a relationship is when someone leaves or abandons you, and you don't have the chance to talk with them and at least get some closure. Please understand if you've been hurt by someone in the past, you do not need to talk with them to have closure – to heal, forgive, and eventually feel at peace inside yourself about the relationship. While it's wonderful when you are able to actually communicate with the person, that can definitely make it easier, if you can't or they are unwilling to do so, fortunately there are other ways that you can find the peace, love, healing or closure that you need. Talking about it with a counselor or coach, writing letters to the other person expressing how you feel—letters that you don't send—are two common ways of finding resolution and peace.

Many of my coaching clients have found the following meditation that I call soul level healing and communication helpful. Close your eyes, get into a relaxed state, and imagine the person you want to communicate with or forgive in your mind's eye. Next imagine your heart center and their heart center—the seat of your souls—filled with light. Finally imagine saying to them whatever you would like to say, knowing that on a soul level, they are receiving your communication.

As human beings we are both human and divine. In other words, you have a human physical self with an ego personality and you also have a divine energetic self or soul. Many people, and I am one of them, believe that you can communicate with another person on a soul level and that their soul will receive your message. Since our souls are not physical but energetic, communication can be received and felt between two souls no matter the distance, time, or space between you. Your communication can be received whether or not the human self and personality of the person you want to communicate with is consciously aware of what's happening. You may even receive communication back from the other person on a soul level, in one of your dreams for example. This can be very healing and bring you peace.

To conclude this section on forgiveness and this chapter, the spiritual text, *A Course in Miracles* says that at the deepest essence there are really only two emotions, love and fear, and that, *"Only the love is real."* What this means is that it is our human personality self with all its pain that acts unloving toward others. On a deeper level, our real self, the part of us that is eternal and always connected to love, would never act unlovingly toward another. When you forgive someone, you are in a sense saying that you forgive them for forgetting who they really are, for acting out of the fear of their wounded human personality self and treating you unlovingly, instead of acting from the truth of who they really are and treating you with love from their divine soul self.

## SECRET FOUR SUMMARY

### How Being in Your Power in Chakra Four Helps You Create the Healthy Love and Life You Want and Deserve

**Health:** Love is what truly heals us, starting with self-love. Loving yourself is healing yourself. Research has shown that when you focus on your heart and on love and gratitude, it strengthens your immune system and calms your nervous system. You then release the relaxing chemicals oxytocin and dopamine which helps you release stress and tension. Listening to your heart is what leads to a happy, fulfilling life, and happiness is also very good for your health. Forgiving yourself and others releases energetic blockages around your heart that prevent you from fully giving and receiving love and brings your whole body back into a state of balance and harmony. Love in all its forms is what heals you and your body.

**Love and relationships:** You can only accept a level of love from another equal to the level of love that you have for yourself. When you learn how to truly love yourself, deeply, completely, and unconditionally, you will attract the same kind of love from a partner, or you will move on from a partner who is not capable of loving you the way you want and deserve. As you change your energy and inner subconscious patterns, you will either see those positive changes reflected in your outer relationships, or you will have the answers and clarity you need to take the next best step for you. When you release past hurts with compassion, understanding and forgiveness, you will keep your heart open and be able to give and receive abundant love in all forms. As you come to realize that your ultimate source of love is always available to you through your own heart and through your connection to your Spiritual Source, you will no longer make someone else your ultimate source which results in codependence and giving your power away. The healthiest, happiest relationships are between two people who love themselves and who want to share their love with each other instead of trying to get the love from each other that they are not giving to themselves.

## CHAKRA FOUR EMPOWERED WOMAN MANTRAS

*I listen to and follow my heart's true desires.*
*I am lovable just as I am.*
*I have a loving relationship with myself.*
*My heart is open.*
*I radiate love.*
*I forgive myself and others.*
*I feel compassion for myself and others.*
*I am overflowing with love.*
*I love myself the way I want to be loved by others.*
*I love myself unconditionally.*
*My true love is either with me now, or on his way to me now.*
*I am one with Divine Love.*
*The love I seek is within me and all around me.*
*I feel so grateful.*

In addition to practicing forgiveness there are two other very important aspects of healthy love that we need to discuss next. These aspects are allowing yourself to be vulnerable and learning how to communicate your feelings and needs in both an empowered and loving way. It's time now to move up to chakra five and secret number five, so you can learn about healthy vulnerability and empowered loving communication.

# EMPOWERED WOMAN
# **SECRET FIVE**

# CHAKRA FIVE

*Empowered Loving Communication, Embracing Your Healthy
Vulnerability and Speaking Your Truth with Love*

# CHAPTER FIVE
# SECRET FIVE

Everything you've learned so far with secrets one through four will help you to step into your power in chakra five. You need the previous four secrets to be an empowered loving communicator. When you're grounded, present, and connected to yourself as we discussed with secret one, you will be more in touch with your feelings so that you can communicate them to others as we discussed in secret two. Releasing and changing any false beliefs especially relating to communication, such as feeling it's not okay for you to ask for what you need, as we discussed with secret three will also help you to be in your power in this fifth chakra. And finally, to be in your power in chakra five you need to communicate with love and from your heart as we discussed with secret four.

The fifth empowered woman secret to creating the healthy love and life you want and deserve is about embracing your vulnerability, practicing empowered loving communication and speaking your truth with love. The location of your fifth chakra is in the center of your throat, which makes perfect sense because this chakra is about communication and self-expression. The color of this chakra is a light blue, like a beautiful blue sky.

## CHAKRA FIVE - IN YOUR POWER

When you are in your power in chakra five, you communicate from your heart, you allow yourself to be vulnerable and authentic, and you're able to communicate your feelings, needs, and boundaries with love. You listen deeply to others with an open mind and an open heart. You are working through any fears or false beliefs that you may have about intimacy, love, or self-expression. For example, if you have a fear about speaking up and telling the truth, you explore the reasons why and do the inner work to help you to release these fears and false beliefs. You're aware of your intention and the energy behind your words and communicate with love from your empowered woman self. Your communication brings you closer to those that you love and care about.

## CHAKRA FIVE - NOT IN YOUR POWER

When you are not in your power in chakra five, you don't express how you really feel because you're uncomfortable being vulnerable. You either hold everything inside, suppressing your emotions and what you want to say, or you do express yourself but you communicate with criticism, judgment, or blame. You may be unaware of your relationship fears, such as the fear of rejection or abandonment and unconsciously push others away with your communication. You emotionally react, rather than respond, and communicate with the energy of fear and insecurity which is the opposite of communicating with the energy of love from your empowered woman self.

## HEALTHY AND UNHEALTHY VULNERABILITY

Vulnerability is about your emotional needs and having an open heart, which is why we discussed it with secrets two and four, but it also relates to how you communicate. *Before we discuss communication in more depth, it's important for you to understand the difference between healthy and unhealthy vulnerability.*

Unhealthy vulnerability is about neediness and emotional reactivity, it's coming from disempowered, codependent energy. Instead of sharing your feelings with the energy of wanting to share and connect, you're sharing them with demands, an agenda, with expectations or to try to control or change someone. Unhealthy vulnerability always comes from fear, neediness, and insecurity. In addition, when you don't have healthy boundaries as we discussed with secret three you will be more "vulnerable" to being taken advantage of or hurt. That would also be considered unhealthy vulnerability.

*In contrast, healthy vulnerability is an open-hearted energy that cultivates true intimacy.* It's about allowing another person into your heart. In other words, it creates a true heart connection with someone. It involves sharing how you feel from your heart. You share your feelings with the intention of connecting with someone instead of sharing with expectations or some kind of agenda, such as trying to change the other person.

When you allow yourself to be truly vulnerable, it is a sign of strength and courage, not weakness or powerlessness which is what society often tells us. It's about being authentic, open, and real. It's heart-centered, and it allows someone to know, support, and hear you. It's not always easy to be vulnerable with someone, especially if you've been hurt, or to trust someone with all of your heart, feelings, and insecurities.

Being hurt as a child or as an adult may have caused you to protect your heart. Have compassion for yourself when your fears and insecurities come up. Remember that you are absolutely loveable and worthy of being with supportive, loving people who really see you and fully love you and accept you as you are. However, you need to do this for yourself also. You need to fall in love with all of you, which includes your strengths and gifts as well as all of your vulnerabilities and insecurities.

*True healthy vulnerability helps you grow in your capacity to love because vulnerability is what leads to emotional intimacy.* You can't avoid the possibility of being hurt when you open your heart, yet at the same time, it allows you to have a deep heart connection with someone. You have to decide if it's worth the risk. It can, of course, bring up fear when you open yourself up to the possibility of being hurt, but what is the alternative? Do you really want to keep the walls up and never have the intimate, loving connection that you want with a partner or with other important people in your life?

To become more comfortable being vulnerable with others, start by being more vulnerable with yourself, which means being honest about how you really feel, what you really need, and what you really desire.

Become aware of your fears, because if you're not, you will be controlled by them, especially in your relationships. For example, many women attract and get into relationships with emotionally unavailable men because they have a fear of being vulnerable and emotionally intimate with a man. It may feel safer to you on a *subconscious level* to be with a man who doesn't have the capability to be emotionally intimate because you won't ever be able to get too close to him and risk getting hurt.

This is why doing the inner work is so important. You want to become aware of what your fears and false beliefs are so you can change and reprogram them as you learned with secret three. You want to be compassionate and loving with yourself when fear arises, but you don't want to let your fears rule you and prevent you from having a loving relationship with a partner or with other loved ones. ***Practicing self-love, as we discussed with secret four, will help you to feel more comfortable being vulnerable.***

## RELEASE YOUR FEARS AND KNOW THAT LOVE IS SAFE

The most common fears of the women I have coached are those of rejection and abandonment. Some women may have other fears as well. We all have some fear about being vulnerable, so again, please have compassion for yourself when those fears arise. Fears of rejection, abandonment or a fear of getting hurt can cause you to feel that love is not safe. Feeling that love is not safe will make it hard to attract love. ***The good news is these fears will decrease when you increase your self-esteem and sense of self-worth.***

If you feel unlovable, unworthy and not good enough, then you would naturally be afraid of intimacy and being vulnerable in a relationship, because you *expect* to be hurt, rejected, etc. When you feel lovable, good enough and have high self-esteem, rather than expecting to be hurt, rejected or abandoned, you are curious about how things will evolve in a relationship and know that whatever happens, you will be okay.

What a man does or doesn't do may cause you to feel disappointed, but it will not cause you to feel negatively about yourself. If a man breaks up with you, for example, you might think and feel, "This means we're not a good match, he's obviously not the right person for me." Whereas if deep down you feel not good enough and unlovable, if a man breaks up with you, you will feel more rejected and feel that something is wrong with you, that you're not worthy or valuable and the painful pattern continues, with you *expecting* to be hurt. ***This is why secret three is so important. You need to change the negative expectations, false beliefs and repetitive painful emotional patterns in your energy and subconscious mind to change the results in your outer world. You need to raise your self-esteem and claim your worthiness from within.***

In addition to feeling unlovable or unworthy of love, many women, as I previously mentioned have the feeling and belief in their subconscious mind that *love isn't safe* because of experiencing hurt in the past. Therefore, you may also need to reprogram your subconscious mind with the truth; *real, true love is safe.* In fact, if it's not safe, it isn't love! ***It's not loving yourself, not having healthy boundaries, and having disempowering relationship patterns that isn't safe, but as you've been learning throughout this book, you can change your patterns! Love itself is completely safe!***

## IS IT OKAY TO "NEED" A MAN OR WANT A RELATIONSHIP?

Some women close down and tell themselves that they don't really need a man. As an empowered woman it's actually okay to need a man. *A healthy, loving man likes to be needed and feel like he is making a valuable contribution to your life, as long as you're not being needy and expecting him to be the ultimate source of your love and happiness.* As we discussed in chapter three, being needy is different than having needs. You want a man to *add* love and happiness to your life, not be the only source of it! ***Having emotional needs is healthy and human, but being needy and codependent is unhealthy and creates problems.***

When some women say they don't need a man, it's really because they are afraid to open their heart or because they feel bitter. They really do want to be close to a man, but they deny that desire because they've been hurt and therefore feel jaded, or they're afraid of being vulnerable. If this sounds like you, remind yourself that you can protect yourself, you can listen to and trust your intuition, and you can set boundaries. ***With healthy boundaries (secret three), you can allow your heart to open and you can work through your fears.***

You can choose to trust and love yourself, allowing your true self to be seen and truly loved. At the same time, this isn't about letting everyone see your vulnerable side; it is about tuning in to your intuition to know who is worthy of seeing your deepest self. It's not safe to share your vulnerable side with some people. If you are tuned in and connected to yourself and your intuition, you'll start to know when and with whom you can be vulnerable.

If you feel bitter, jaded or negative about men or relationships in general, review the relationship spiritual truths and forgiveness sections in chapter four. As human beings we have a need for closeness and intimacy with other humans. It's been proven that we are wired to connect and bond with others. *Wanting a relationship is a healthy emotional need and desire, so embrace your desire to have a loving relationship with a partner!*

If it wasn't safe for you to express your feelings and to be vulnerable growing up, it may be challenging for you to do it as an adult. But now as an empowered woman, you can choose to open your heart and let down those walls you built out of fear. *The more you release the past and program into your subconscious mind that love is safe, the more you'll be able to be vulnerable with others.*

Yes, there is always a possibility of being hurt, betrayed, rejected, or abandoned. The question is are you going to let that stop you from letting a man into your heart and from having an intimate loving relationship? Keep in mind, when you're vulnerable, it allows or invites the person you're with to open up and be vulnerable with you also. Author Brene Brown writes about the power of vulnerability and how it's what creates an emotional connection with others. Sometimes you can bond deeply with someone when you allow them to help you at a vulnerable point in your life. This happened to me once with a new friendship. I was sick and feeling vulnerable, and a co-worker friend came over and helped me. This made me feel closer to her, and as a result, we became closer friends.

In other words, when you're vulnerable with your partner or others it usually helps them feel more comfortable opening up and being vulnerable with you too. *If you don't show any vulnerability in a relationship, you won't feel an emotional connection with the person because emotional intimacy requires vulnerability.*

## EMPATHY AND VULNERABILITY

*Having empathy for someone's feelings also requires vulnerability.* To relate in this deep way, you need to be in touch with your own feelings. Again, vulnerability, as uncomfortable or scary as it can feel sometimes, is the key to emotional intimacy. Healthy vulnerability usually involves facing your fears, choosing to open up and trust a special someone with your heart, your insecurities, and your imperfections. It's a great feeling when we know that someone loves us regardless of all our quirks and imperfections. The question is do you love yourself with all your quirks and imperfections? Remember, we must love ourselves the way we want to be loved by another. And the more you love yourself and feel worthy and deserving of love from others, the less fear and negative expectations you will have about men, intimacy and relationships. *Keep loving yourself and reminding yourself that love is safe.*

## SPEAKING YOUR TRUTH WITH LOVE

The more comfortable you are with being vulnerable, the more you'll be able to speak your truth with love and communicate in an empowered and loving way. When you can allow yourself to be honest, open, real, and vulnerable, you can speak your truth with love, which is speaking with empowered loving communication.

Most women were not taught how to do this. They were either taught to stay silent, not speak up and be the nice girl or to communicate with aggressiveness or harshness, i.e., with criticism, judgment and blame. The key to communicating as an empowered woman is to speak your truth with love. When something is bothering you, do you either keep your feelings inside or blurt something out that is harsh and therefore not received well? Very often, the problem is not what you say, but how you say it. The actual words you say are very important, but your non-verbal communication is even more important—the tone of your voice, your facial expression, your body language, etc. *These convey your intention and the energy behind your words, and they are what others feel and respond to, even if they aren't consciously aware of it.*

There is an art to tuning in to your feelings and learning how to communicate them. Learning how to speak with love doesn't mean that you're watering down what you have to say, because love is very powerful. *When you speak your truth with the energy of love most people will feel and respond positively to it.*

Keep in mind that communicating and speaking your truth with love is a learned skill that takes practice, so please don't be hard on yourself or expect perfection. Don't put pressure on yourself by worrying that you will make a mistake. Be forgiving of yourself and others. *If you're working toward becoming more conscious of the way you communicate, you are on the path of being an empowered woman.*

## HOW MEN RESPOND WHEN WOMEN EXPRESS THEIR EMOTIONS

Most women don't have trouble communicating when they feel happy and peaceful, but when we are emotionally triggered it often becomes challenging to communicate with love. There is a big myth that most men don't like it when women express their emotions or get too emotional. This is simply not true. It's how you communicate your emotions and the energy behind what you share that can push men away, not your feelings and emotions themselves. Men often get defensive and don't want to listen if as you communicate how you feel, you're making them wrong, blaming them, making them responsible for your feelings, or criticizing them. This applies to people in general, but especially to men. *The important thing to know when it comes to communication is how to communicate your feelings without criticism, judgment, or blame.*

Communicating without criticism, judgment, or blame and expressing how you really feel and what you need or want requires vulnerability, which is why I discussed vulnerability first. If you're having some challenges in a relationship, be curious and compassionate. Everyone is doing the best they can. If someone is doing something that bothers you, rather than judge them, be curious as to the reasons why they are doing what they are doing. When you are in your heart (instead of in your head judging someone) and you ask questions with curiosity and love, you will learn a lot about the other person.

*It's important to understand that most men and women have different vulnerabilities.* Men are wired to want to succeed and win, so their core vulnerability is to feel like they are failing, while the core vulnerability for women is to feel like we are not loved. If a man feels like he is failing with you, he will close down and won't be able to hear anything you're saying. *Men will avoid situations where they feel like they are failing and not winning or where they feel incompetent.*

If the energy beneath your words is saying, "You did something wrong and you're failing," (remember you're not actually saying those words but that is the energy behind your words), he will likely get defensive and will not want to listen to you express your emotions. If he is defensive, it means he is protecting himself. *If he feels like he has to protect himself from you, he will not be able to hear what you have to say.*

If you want to know how a man is feeling emotionally, remember that thinking is masculine energy and feeling is feminine energy. Even though both men and women think and feel, when it comes to communicating, try asking a man what he thinks about something first before asking him how he feels. Men love it when you ask them what they think and when you respect their thinking, even if you have a different point of view. Asking a man what he thinks often invites him to start opening up emotionally, which is a good thing because many men are not as in touch with their feelings as women are, as I'm sure many of you have noticed!

## EMPOWERED LOVING COMMUNICATION

It's important to understand the energetics of communication and learn how to communicate with love so that a man or any other person in your life can actually hear you. As an empowered woman you do not need to attack, blame, make someone wrong, nag, complain, or try to control someone to get what you want. When you're feeling emotionally triggered, you want to go within and ask yourself what you are really feeling, needing, or wanting and then think about how you can communicate that with love.

If you communicate with a man or anyone else when you are angry, upset, or highly triggered, it's not going to go well. There is no point in communicating with that kind of energy.

As an empowered woman you are the master of your emotions, which often means you don't act on them right away. If you do, you could find yourself texting, emailing, calling, or saying things you'll later wish you hadn't said. When this happens, you'll know that you haven't processed your own emotions and that you communicated your feelings too soon.

*If you're highly emotionally triggered, you're most likely going to communicate with the energy of fear, not love. Trying to get love, empathy or understanding from a man or anyone from an uncentered, unloving place does not work.* Instead, pause, tune in, and get centered. Don't just blurt out the first thing that you want to say. You aren't going to deny how you feel and keep everything inside; you're just going to go within and really tune in and connect with yourself first. *You are in your power when you are communicating honestly from your heart and with the energy of love.*

You are not in your power when you communicate when you are too emotionally triggered and reactive. Don't deny your emotions, but feel them and try to understand where they are coming from. In order to process and work through them, you need to love and comfort yourself. Then you'll be more able to communicate with love from your empowered woman self.

*Your power is always in love.* The paradox is that when you get in touch with the vulnerable part of you or your inner little girl and you attend to her needs, validate her feelings, and love her, then you can truly step into your power as an adult woman and speak your truth with love. After comforting or reassuring the fearful, emotionally reactive part of you, when you are ready to communicate, *be sure to tell a man what you like or love and ask for what you want, rather than focusing on what you don't like and don't want with your communication. In addition, please remember to communicate whatever you're grateful for and express your appreciation for what he is doing right!*

Focusing on what you don't like and don't want can feel like criticism and bring up those feelings of failure in a man. Focusing on and communicating what you like, love, and want tells him what he can do to make you feel good and bring you happiness. Deep down, even if he's not consciously aware of it, this is what a good, loving man wants in a relationship.

*He wants to feel successful at bringing you happiness, he wants to feel like he's making an important and needed contribution in your life. He wants to feel like he's winning with you! Please remember this when you communicate with someone you're dating, with a partner or with any man in your life.*

## THE ENERGY UNDERNEATH YOUR COMMUNICATION

Good communication is all about tuning in to your own needs and heart's desires and then asking or telling your partner what you need and want in a loving, empowered way. This is not about being a doormat or not having boundaries. As an empowered woman you have healthy boundaries as we discussed in chapter three, and will discuss again shortly, but you are setting boundaries with love. You are not criticizing, blaming, whining, being needy, complaining, begging, or trying to control.

So ask yourself before you express your feelings if what you want to say is coming from a needy, insecure, fearful, emotionally reactive place and energy or is it coming from the energy of love and a sense of your own worthiness. In other words, is what you are about to say coming from codependent, disempowered energy or from your empowered woman self who knows what you really want and deserve because you love and respect yourself. *A man will feel the difference between the two and respond to the energy behind your words.*

You want your energy to communicate self-confidence. As a self-confident woman, you feel that it would be wonderful if a particular man can give you what you want and deserve, but if not, you know that you are going to be okay and you are willing to walk away. You do not want to communicate with disempowered feminine energy, i.e., with the energy of fear, neediness and insecurity. *In other words, you do not want your energy to communicate that you need him to do something so that you can feel worthy, valuable and lovable. That would be giving your power away because you are worthy, valuable and lovable no matter what any man does or doesn't do!*

## YOUR FEELINGS AND NEEDS ARE IMPORTANT

Communicating with love does not mean that you don't ever feel angry. You can communicate anything with love, including anger. When you communicate from a centered, empowered, honest, truthful, loving place in your heart, and you're not attacking the other person, they will pay much more attention to whatever it is that you have to say and will be less likely to get defensive.

People you care about, including your partner, are not perfect, and they may sometimes do things that hurt or upset you. If you feel hurt and you're not sure how to respond, sometimes a great thing to say is simply, "Ouch, that hurt," then just pause and wait for the reaction. Notice that you're not focusing on the other person at all. You're just communicating that you were hurt. You're being vulnerable, but you're not going into anger and blame and making them wrong. If you speak from your heart with honesty, love, and vulnerability and the other person has no empathy for you, that is a big warning sign. *You want and deserve to be with someone who is capable of empathy. Your feelings need to be as important to him as his feelings are to you.*

Some women are afraid that if they express their feelings, they might come across as needy and push a man away. They may shut down and withdraw because they have a fear of rejection or abandonment. As an empowered woman, you know that your needs and feelings are important and you will express them honestly even though there may be a part of you that is afraid that you will lose the other person. Be willing to face that fear. Remind yourself that it's better to lose someone else than to lose yourself. Don't fall into the trap of attempting to keep a relationship by trying to be someone that you're not. If you're not expressing your true feelings and who you truly are, your relationship is based on a false premise. *You won't be able to experience true intimacy if you're hiding your true feelings and not being yourself.*

## COMMUNICATING AND LISTENING WITH LOVE

Validation and empathy are the two most essential heart-felt components of empowered loving communication. They can be incredibly healing and helpful in all kinds of relationships, especially our most intimate ones. Before discussing how to communicate your boundaries with love and assertiveness, there are three very important components of both communicating and listening with love. These components are validation, empathy and empathic listening, which is the deepest form of listening. Please keep these components in mind and include them whenever you can when you are communicating or listening to others. You may be quite surprised at how helpful and healing they can be.

**1 -VALIDATION**: Validation is acknowledging another person's experience, thoughts, or opinions. Examples: "I know that you've been under a lot of stress lately," or, "You don't think what your boss said is fair." When you validate the other person, you're letting them know that you hear them, and that you see them and where they are. In essence you're saying, "I get what you're thinking or experiencing." You're not passing judgment on the other person's experience—you're just the witness, and your mind is open.

**2 -EMPATHY**: Empathy is the ability to understand and share the feelings of another. Example: "I understand and know how you feel, that must be so painful." Expressing empathy is letting someone know that you understand how they are feeling. In a sense you are also validating how they feel. Validation and empathy are often interconnected, but the key thing is when you express them, you're not attempting to fix or change how the other person thinks or feels. With empathy, you're standing beside them, feeling compassion as they express their feelings. There's no judgement and your heart is open.

**3 - EMPATHIC LISTENNG:** The deepest from of listening to another person is often called empathic listening. With empathic listening you are fully present with no distractions or judgment. Your heart is open, and you are listening not just to someone's words but also for the feelings underneath their words. You are not listening to come up with a reply; you are simply listening to understand the other person, not so you can give them advice or debate with them. You are listening to get to know them, to hear them. You are listening to understand and validate their thoughts, which does not mean that you have to agree with them, but you do acknowledge where they are coming from. You are listening to understand and to have empathy for their feelings.

*If you're not sure you understand something that is being said to you and you want clarification, you can use paraphrasing which is also called reflecting.* With paraphrasing, you repeat back to someone what they just said to you in your own words. Then you ask them if what you heard them say is correct and if the emotions you are sensing from them are in fact what they are feeling. Sometimes the greatest gift you can give someone is to truly listen to them deeply in this way. Many people have not been listened to in this way throughout their life, and it can be incredibly healing.

Now that we have discussed empowered loving communication in general, let's talk specifically about how to communicate your boundaries. With secret three we discussed the importance of *having* healthy boundaries, now it's time to learn how to *communicate* your boundaries with both love and assertiveness.

## COMMUNICATING BOUNDARIES WITH LOVE AND ASSERTIVENESS

There are four basic communication styles. One of them, the assertive style, will help you communicate your boundaries with love and respect for yourself and others. The other three do not support healthy, good communication. Notice when you are using these three communication styles so that you can bring yourself back to assertiveness as soon as possible. Here are the four styles.

**Passive** – You feel your needs, feelings and desires are not very important, at least not as important as everyone else's. You either don't speak up, keeping your feelings and thoughts inside, or worse, you're not even aware of how you feel and allow other people to make decisions for you. You tend to take on too much responsibility for a communication interaction and apologize often. You have difficulty setting boundaries and lack self-esteem.

**Aggressive** - You feel your needs, feelings and desires are more important than everyone else's, and you communicate with criticism, judgment and blame. You do not take responsibility for your part in communication interactions. You are defensive and self-absorbed and may not respect other people's boundaries. You communicate with a lot of "you" messages. This style also shows a lack of self-esteem.

**Passive-Aggressive** – You appear to be passive on the surface, but you are indirectly communicating aggressively. This often involves being manipulative and trying to make the other person feel guilty in order to get what you want. Like the passive and aggressive styles, you are not in your power here and you lack confidence and self-esteem.

**Assertive Communication** – This is the healthiest style of communication, and it is characteristic of someone with high self-esteem. You are direct and honest with kindness. You are loving and not harsh. You speak with "I" messages and take responsibility for your own emotions. You know how you feel and what you need or want. You feel that your needs and desires are important, but you also respect the other person's needs and desires. You are able to set healthy boundaries and you respect the boundaries of others.

Communicating your boundaries with love and assertive communication usually involves three steps. If you want someone to be receptive to what you're going to say, then follow these steps:

**Step One** - Express some empathy, validate the other person and/or show appreciation.

**Step Two** - Express how you feel. Share what feelings the other person's behavior or the situation brings up for you. You're not attacking them as a person, but you are expressing what came up for you when they did or didn't do or say something, etc.

**Step Three** - Ask or tell the other person what you need or want.

Here is an example illustrating all three steps:

You're at a social function with your boyfriend when he becomes irritated with you for something and snaps at you in front of other people. This does not feel good to you so you decide to speak to him and set a boundary. Later that night you talk with him about it.

**Step One - Expressing empathy, validation or appreciation:** "I really appreciate that you came to the party with me. I know you've been under a lot of stress lately, and that you didn't mean to hurt me or startle me, and… (use the word "and" instead of the words "but" or "however" because those words will negate what you just said in step one)

**Step Two – Expressing and taking responsibility for how you feel:** "When you snapped at me in front of other people, I felt uncomfortable." You are describing his behavior and using an "I" message to share and take responsibility for your feelings.

**Step Three – Express or ask for whatever it is that you want or need**: "In the future, if you are upset with me, rather than snapping at me especially in front of others, can you please talk with me about whatever is upsetting you when we are alone together?" This can be said as a statement of what you want or as a question. It really depends on the nature of your relationship and many other factors.

## COLLABORATIVE COMMUNICATION

Another example of empowered loving communication is a collaborative style of communicating. Let's say that your partner has been playing a lot of golf on the weekends and you miss him. You could say something like "I know you have been under a lot of stress lately and that golfing helps you to release stress, and at the same time I've really been missing you and feeling a desire to have more time with you. ***Can we talk about this tonight and come up with a way for both of us to get our needs met, for you to release stress with golf and for me to have more time and connection with you?***"

*Notice how you are collaborating with him and asking for his help in solving a problem*. Most men like to solve problems, so this collaboration method of communication is often very helpful and effective. Can you see how when you communicate in this way that you're not making him wrong for golfing too much? If you tell him that he is golfing too much, and you complain about it, it will create the opposite result of what you want. It's not just *what* you say that's important, but *how* you say it that really matters. ***Men and people in general will feel and respond to the energy beneath your words.***

## WHEN SOMEONE IS NOT RESPECTING YOUR BOUNDARIES

Keep in mind that your boundaries are your own and unique to you. Someone else may not be bothered by what your boyfriend did. The key is, if you're not okay with it, then you need to speak up. If someone isn't respecting your boundaries, that's definitely not a good sign, and depending upon the nature of the relationship, you may want to let them know what the consequences will be if their behavior continues. ***By consequence, I mean what you are going to do to take of yourself.***

***Setting boundaries is not about the other person. It's not about telling them what to do, controlling them, punishing them or threatening them.*** If you've told someone how you feel and set a boundary, but they keep doing the same thing, then you may want to let them know what you are going to do to take care of or protect yourself. For example, if your soon to be ex-husband is yelling at you on the phone and you've asked him to please stop raising his voice, but he keeps doing it, then you could tell him that if he continues to yell, that you are going to have to hang up the phone (the consequence), because the yelling is ***not okay with you.***

Your energy behind your words should *not* be communicating, "I'm trying to change or control you and your behavior or threaten you." Instead, you are simply telling him what you need to do and what you will in fact be doing to protect and take care of yourself. This will give the other person a chance to look at themselves and change their behavior. ***If they don't despite knowing the consequences, then you have just learned something about this person and about your relationship.***

## SECRET FIVE SUMMARY

### How Empowered Woman Secret Number Five Helps You Create the Healthy Love and Life You Want and Deserve

**Health:** A big part of having boundaries is being able to communicate them with love. If you don't have boundaries or you are afraid to communicate them, you can become physically or emotionally drained by your relationships. This can negatively affect your health. If you do not communicate assertively, you may find yourself in situations that are even harmful to you and your health. Communicating how you honestly think and feel and asking for what you need and want are acts of self-love and self-care—and self-love is healing for your body, heart, and soul.

**Love and Relationships:** Healthy vulnerability is essential to emotional intimacy and to having a heart connection with others, and communication is a very important part of love and relationships! I cannot emphasize enough the importance of how you communicate, not only the words, but especially the energy and intention behind your words, for that is what people really feel. When you communicate with love, authenticity and healthy vulnerability instead of with needy demands, criticism, judgment, or blame, your relationships with others will likely deepen and improve. You can't control how other people respond to you, you can only do your part, but you have the best chance of resolving conflicts or disagreements and having truly healthy, intimate relationships with others when you practice empowered loving communication and empathic listening.

## CHAKRA FIVE EMPOWERED WOMAN MANTRAS:

*I speak my truth with love.*
*I embrace my vulnerability and communicate from my heart.*
*I communicate from my empowered woman self.*
*I communicate my boundaries with love.*
*I express who I really am.*
*I express myself clearly, confidently, and authentically.*
*I express my true feelings easily and naturally.*
*My communication brings me closer to those that I love and care about.*
*I allow myself to be seen, heard and known.*
*I know who to trust with my vulnerability.*
*I listen to others with an open mind and an open heart.*

*It takes time to become an empowered woman communicator, so be patient with yourself and know that you will have many opportunities to practice and improve your communication skills! I could write an entire book on communication, but we must move on now to empowered woman secret number six.*

# EMPOWERED WOMAN
## SECRET SIX

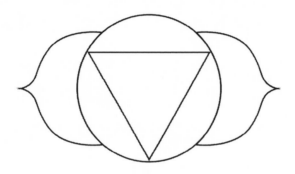

# CHAKRA SIX

*Manifesting Your Heart's Desires with Your Intuition,
Imagination and Empowered Feminine Energy*

# CHAPTER SIX
# SECRET SIX

The sixth empowered woman secret to creating the healthy love and life you want and deserve is about magnetically manifesting what you want with your intuition, imagination and empowered feminine energy. Chakra six is located in the center of your forehead and is often referred to as your third eye. It is the chakra that is most often associated with intuition, even though your second and fourth chakras are also powerful intuitive centers. It is associated with the power of your imagination and seeing things from a higher, spiritual perspective. The color of this center is a deep midnight blue called indigo.

## CHAKRA SIX - IN YOUR POWER

When you are in your power in your sixth chakra, you're able to imagine the kind of relationship and life you want and you commit to that vision. You know that you are the creative artist of your life. You're in touch with and listen to your intuition, allowing it to guide you as you manifest your desires. You can see things from the higher perspective of your soul, especially when you are experiencing challenges.

## CHAKRA SIX - NOT IN YOUR POWER

When you're not in your power here, you will be out of touch with your intuition, making it harder to manifest what you want. You may not see yourself and others clearly, meaning that you may be in some form of denial. You lack clarity and are not able to imagine the kind of love and life you want and have difficulty seeing things from the higher spiritual perspective of your soul.

## MANIFESTATION AND THE "LAW OF ATTRACTION"

Before we begin, I want to define what I mean by manifestation and briefly discuss my perspective on the law of attraction that we have all heard so much about since the publication of the book, *The Secret*. Manifestation is creating, attracting or bringing something into your life that you want. As a woman, you have more power than you realize to manifest what your heart desires. I believe that even if something seems unlikely, all things, including your love and life dreams, are possible. Not everyone believes this because most people view things from a victim consciousness, thinking that they have no control over what's happening to them and taking no responsibility for their lives. In recent years, after the popularity of the movie *The Secret*, many people began to take more personal responsibility and some embraced the idea that they were "creating their reality" with their thoughts and consciousness.

Although I believe this idea can be empowering—and it is certainly better than victim consciousness—I've seen many people take it way too far. Instead of taking some responsibility for their lives, they blame and judge themselves. When things don't go well, they feel a sense of shame, like they did something wrong and that what happened or is happening is their fault. This is not a healthy, helpful, or an accurate way of looking at things. Such beliefs also seem to bring up an issue that many of us have deep down, which the desire to control everything. We can certainly do our part and align the energy of our thoughts, emotions, and consciousness with the highest and best possible outcome, but as you have probably figured out, we cannot control everything that happens to us or around us.

*We all know that life is not always predictable.* It seems more accurate to say that we are creating our experience of reality by how we choose to respond to what happens in our lives. We can choose our attitude, how we are going to perceive things, the actions we take, and what we are going to believe, as we discussed with secret three.

*Yes, our thoughts, energy, and emotions definitely help to create our lives, as we will be discussing in this chapter, but the tricky thing is, most of this is happening on a subconscious level, rather than with conscious choice and awareness.* In other words, when you have challenges you are usually not consciously wanting or creating them! And remember, your subconscious mind is really like your inner child because it holds those feelings and beliefs from the first six or seven years of your life, so please have compassion for yourself. Your subconscious is 90% of your mind. Therefore, the more conscious you become of the thoughts, beliefs, and emotions in your subconscious mind, the better. You will have more power to create the healthy love and life you want when you become aware of the subconscious blocks that have been preventing you from manifesting what you consciously desire. With that awareness you will then be able to consciously choose new thoughts, emotions, and beliefs, make new choices and release disempowering behavior patterns, but this may take time, so please be patient and kind to yourself.

*When things are difficult for you or they aren't happening exactly when and how you would like, it's a really good time to look at your current circumstances from a higher, more spiritual perspective.* One way to do this is to ask yourself what your soul might be wanting to learn through whatever challenge you may be experiencing. If you think of the earth as a school that we souls attend to learn about love, to grow, and to gain wisdom, what classes does it seem like you have you signed up for? What kind of earth diploma are you working on?

Learning how to love myself and how to become a more empowered woman has been a big part of my life's curriculum. In this book, I'm sharing what I've learned with the intention of teaching and empowering you and as many other women as possible. My mother had an earth curriculum that involved learning about self-love and self-empowerment also. Toward the end of her life, she was definitely discovering how to love herself and how to become a more empowered woman. She was a very courageous woman for her time, yet the challenges I watched her go through as I was growing up and her long battle with cancer before she died when I was a very young woman, had a very painful and profound effect on me. *At the same time, it became the inspiration for my life's work. When you look at your life from a higher perspective, you can find meaning even in your most painful and challenging life experiences.*

Please know that it's wonderful to hold the vision and intention for what you want to bring into your life, which is part of what we will be discussing in this chapter with secret six, but it is not helpful to think that you can control everything and then blame yourself for your challenges. I believe that the Divine Loving Intelligence of the Universe does respond to our intentions and heart-felt desires, but have you noticed that despite your best intentions, things don't always happen when or how you want them to? Very often, we are faced with obstacles and challenges before we manifest what we want. This is actually part of the process and why we need to see things from our soul's higher perspective and cultivate faith. I believe that we are co-creating our life with the higher power of our Spiritual Source, a topic that will be discussed in chapter seven. In this chapter you're going to learn about your part in this co-creative manifestation process and specifically how to help create what you want and deserve using your intuition, imagination and empowered feminine energy.

## MANIFESTING WITH YOUR EMPOWERED FEMININE ENERGY

Most people are very familiar with how to use masculine power and energy to manifest what they want. You set a goal, break it down into steps, strategize, and create a plan to achieve it. Sometimes this works well, but other times, there may be challenges using just this masculine energy goal-setting strategy. *When your subconscious mind is in conflict with your conscious mind's goal and desire, masculine power alone is not enough.* The masculine goal setting strategy alone works best for more concrete things like building a house, buying a car etc., but it may not work as well when what you want to create is something like having a healthy, loving relationship, a healthier body, or a happier life. Manifesting these things is not just a linear process.

*When you create with your feminine power your empowered masculine energy supports your empowered feminine energy. Here's how they work together:*

**1** - Manifesting with your empowered feminine energy involves first going into your heart (instead of just your head's masculine energy) and asking yourself if what you want to create is your true heart's desire. When what you think you want is coming just from your head or from what you think you "should" do or what other people think you "should" do, you won't find the happiness you seek. As I've said, your heart is what guides you to true fulfillment.

**2** - You do want to set a clear intention for what you want and then believe that it is possible for you to have it, such as, "I want to attract my ideal life partner." Setting your intention and the direction you're going to go is masculine energy, but your true desire comes from the yearnings in your heart (your feminine energy). Next, rather than just strategizing and planning (masculine energy), you also need to practice cultivating the feelings and emotions of already having what you desire (feelings and emotions are feminine energy) and then allow your intuition to guide you as far as what actions to take. *In other words, taking action toward what you want is masculine energy, but you want that action to come from and be inspired by your intuition (your empowered feminine energy) versus coming only from your analytical mind, logic, and strategizing.*

**3** - You can use your thinking mind or masculine energy to identify your blocks, false beliefs, and any resistance to having what you want. Then for the actual healing or releasing of these blocks and false beliefs you reprogram your subconscious mind with uplifting emotions which is a feminine energy, heart process. Healing is emotional and spiritual, not logical. As you continue manifesting with your empowered feminine energy, let go of and surrender your attachment to the outcome of your actions (more on this with secret seven), trust the process and allow things to unfold. Trusting and allowing is your empowered feminine energy, as we have discussed in earlier chapters. To say it a bit differently, you will be utilizing the power of your mind (your masculine energy) to manifest what you want, but it is the power of your emotions (your feminine energy) that actually magnetizes and brings what you want to you.

## ALLOWING YOUR LIGHT TO SHINE

*The more you focus on your heart, on love and on how you want to feel in a relationship and in life, the more your inner light will shine and help attract what you want.* As you do the inner work of shifting your energy with self-love and follow the practices in this book, you are learning what dims your light and what allows your light to shine brighter. The brighter your light, the more magnetic you become. What allows your light to shine brighter are many of the things you learned about in the first five chapters. Having high self-esteem and self-worth, setting boundaries, being able to trust, being grounded, feeling a sense of safety and security within yourself, being in your body, loving your body, staying in touch with your feelings and needs, being present in your second chakra, staying connected to your heart, mastering your emotions, awakening and embracing your empowered feminine energy and listening to your intuition all help your light to shine brighter.

## YOU ARE A MAGNETIC WOMAN

As a woman, you are an electromagnetic being. Your thoughts are the electric part, they are like signals that you send out into the universe. "This is what I want; this is what I believe I can have." It's important for you to get as clear as you can about what kind of man, what kind of relationship, what kind of body or health and what kind of life that you want. *Your heart and your feelings (your empowered feminine energy) are the magnetic part; your emotions attract what you want to you.* Remember, your heart creates a magnetic field around your body and so when you bring your attention into your heart you're actually amplifying this field. When that happens, you will have a stronger ability to magnetize and attract to you whatever it is that you are seeking.

*Your feminine energy is also about ease and being in the flow, while your masculine energy is about having a specific direction.* Many of us have been taught that we have to make things happen and that we really need to struggle, work hard and do, do, do to achieve everything we want. Doing is masculine energy and yes, taking action toward your dreams is necessary, but who you are *being* (feminine energy) is equally as important when it comes to manifesting what you want in love and life.

Imagine that manifesting with your empowered feminine energy is like stepping into the flow of a loving intelligence and lifeforce energy and that the Universe is going to bring to you everything that you need. You are open to receive from the Universe and your Spiritual Source. This doesn't mean that you're not going to be taking action; of course, you'll be doing that also, but you want to cultivate the overall attitude, belief, and feeling that you don't have to *struggle* to make everything happen. You can be in the flow and open to the possibility of what you want coming easily. You will be taking action, but from a place of, "Yes, this feels right to do, or yes, I feel really guided to do this."

As you get in touch with your feelings and your intuition ideas will come to you, and you'll know what step to take next. Being in the flow means that you don't have to force anything. *The manifesting process is not about forcing or controlling; it's about relaxing and being open and receptive as you allow your intuition and feelings to be an equal partner with your intellect and logic.*

## YOU ARE THE CREATIVE ARTIST OF YOUR LIFE

Everything you create starts with a desire in your heart and an idea or vision in your imagination. Think of your life as a canvas and you as the artist. Close your eyes and imagine the kind of body and health you want, the kind of relationship you desire, and the kind of life that you want to live. The desires that you have in your heart are there for a reason. *You wouldn't have a dream if it wasn't at least possible to manifest it.*

If you are the artist of your life then the next question is, what is it that you want to create? A mutually loving partner and relationship? Better health? Start with your desire, your dream, then cultivate the belief that what you want is possible. Think about all of the wonderful things, people and experiences that you have already manifested and brought into your life!

Remember what we discussed about the power of your heart. One of the keys to manifesting is to consistently be in a state of high vibration, as we will discuss shortly. When you feel joy and gratitude in your heart, you are vibrating at a very high frequency. One of the best ways to feel this joy is to do things that you love and focus on things for which you are grateful. Believe in your dreams and your heart's desires, and as you start taking action toward them, notice the synchronicities, those signs from the Universe that you are on the right track. You possess something very powerful that is always with you to guide you, and that is your intuition. Let's dive in now to the topic of your women's intuition.

## WOMEN'S INTUITION

*As a woman, you are naturally very intuitive, even though you might not always be very tuned in or aware of it.* As you practice everything you learn in this book you will become more aware of and connected to your intuition. There are four primary kinds of intuitive guidance that you may receive. While you may be intuitive in all four ways, most women are stronger in one or two of the following ways.

### Clairsentience or Empathic Intuition

This type of intuition is connected with your *second chakra* because it is about feelings and emotional energy. This is definitely a strong one for me. With empathic intuition, you can easily feel the emotions and energy of other people and the environment. Women with strong empathic intuition make excellent counselors and coaches, and even if you are not a counselor or coach by profession, people will often open up to you easily and tell you about their problems. You can walk into a room and feel the emotional energy in the air. You can sense what other people are feeling whether in a group or individually.

A lot of people think that being an empath and having strong empathic intuition means that you absorb and take on other people's emotions, but that only happens when you are not in your power. If this happens to you, it is something you need to work on. You need emotional boundaries because you don't want to absorb other people's emotions. I discussed this some in chapters one and two when we talked about staying grounded and mastering your emotions. Also, because your second chakra is your feminine power center, it is naturally a place of deep intuitive wisdom. Remember it is like your second heart, and it will give you intuitive guidance when you are present, tuned in, and seated on your "queen's throne" as we discussed with secret two. Place a hand or two on your second chakra and bring your attention there, then ask a question and be open to receiving an answer.

## Clairvoyance

This second kind of intuition is related to your *sixth chakra.* With clairvoyant intuition, you receive guidance through images that come into your mind or from your nighttime dreams.

## Clairaudience

The third kind of intuition is called clairaudience and is connected to your *fifth chakra.* With clairaudience you receive intuitive messages as if someone is speaking to you in your head. This may seem like a thought, but it doesn't come from your logical mind; it comes from your intuition, and it is the voice of your soul or spirit. For example, you may hear a voice that tells you that you need to drive down a different street, even though you're not aware of any logical reason for you to do so, only later to find out that you would have been stuck in a major traffic jam had you not listened to the voice of your intuitive guidance.

## Claircognizance

The fourth kind of intuition is sometimes called claircognizance, but a better name and description of it is *your inner knowing.* It is associated with your fourth chakra—your heart chakra. You can tap into this inner knowing by tuning in and connecting with your heart on a regular basis. Your heart, as we have discussed in earlier chapters, is a powerful center of intuitive guidance and intelligence. When an empowered woman feels something intuitively in her heart, she usually describes it as an inner knowing. You know something but you don't know how you know it because it's not logical.

A very powerful thing to do, especially if you are like me and your two strongest forms of intuition are connected with your second and fourth chakras, is to place one hand on your heart (chakra four) and one on your lower belly (chakra two) and feel the strong connection between these two feminine power centers. Bring your attention down from your head and into these two hearts. ***Tuning in to both of them together will often give you the guidance and answers you need.***

Begin to notice how your intuition communicates and comes through to you. Your intuition is beyond your rational mind. The more you tune in and pay attention to it and connect with it, the stronger it will become.

## BLOCKS TO INTUITION

Let's discuss now what can block your intuition and what can help it to become stronger. The first thing that can block your intuition is unprocessed emotions. Emotional energy that is stuck, shut down, pushed away, or denied can not only create energy blockages in your body and negatively affect your health, but it can also get in the way of your ability to connect with your intuition. It's like having a clogged drain, and your intuition, which is the way your soul communicates with you, can't get through.

The second thing that can block your intuition is a very harsh inner critic which many women have. If you criticize yourself a lot and you have low self-esteem, that critical voice will block your intuition because it has a very low energy vibration. The higher your vibration is, the more in touch you will be with your intuition.

The third reason that your intuition can become blocked is that you are ungrounded. When you're not grounded, the energy in your body rises up and out of you causing you to feel anxious. To tune in and receive guidance from your intuition, you need to focus your awareness inside of you and be grounded and present in your body.

## STRENGTHENING YOUR INTUITION

Allowing yourself to feel your feelings as they arise and being honest about how you feel, rather than pushing them away is a great way to strengthen your intuition. The more you connect with your body and your feelings, the stronger your intuition will become because sometimes your feelings and intuition are interconnected. I'm sure you've heard the phrase, "I just had a gut feeling," this is your intuition coming through to you as *feelings in your body*. Your intuition does not come from your logical mind or your emotions; it comes from a deeper wisdom and a higher part of you. ***It is the voice of your soul.***

Processing old emotions, old hurts, and emotional baggage will also strengthen your intuition. These can create energy blockages and cloud your intuition. Sometimes this emotional processing is difficult to do on your own. If you need help working through old hurts and trauma, invest in yourself by seeking professional help.

***Another way to increase your intuitive abilities is to allow yourself to take some time to relax and rest, whether it's with some form of meditation or just lying down and listening to some relaxing music.*** Obviously, if you are constantly running or rushing around, always very busy with your external life, you won't be very in touch with your intuition. Instead, prioritize spending some time with yourself and going within. Time spent focusing on your inner self and your inner life will definitely help you to strengthen your intuition.

A final suggestion for increasing your intuitive abilities is to connect with and tune into your heart as much as possible as we discussed in chapter four. Your heart center is connected with your inner knowing, so bringing your attention to your heart as often as you can will help you to tune in to that deep place of wisdom inside.

***Intuition is like a muscle that you develop, but you don't have to work hard at it. Rather you want to relax and allow yourself to slow down and tune in.*** It's not something that you have to try hard to connect with, it will develop naturally when you begin to practice the things that I just mentioned and when you get more in touch with your empowered feminine energy. You just need to be open and receptive (your feminine energy) and allow your intuition to come through with the guidance it wants to give you.

***Always remember that the answers you seek are within you.*** Even if you consult a psychic, as some of you may occasionally do, please do not give your power away thinking someone else knows more than you do about yourself and your own life! A good reading should complement your own intuition while giving you some clarity, insight, confirmation, and a spiritual perspective rather than giving you "answers" and predictions. I have several card decks, from angel cards to cards about love, healing, women's wisdom, and even the chakras that do just that. You always have options, choices and free will. If you are looking for answers in a set of cards or a psychic, you are looking in the wrong place, for deep down you already have the answers inside you. Let psychics, cards, runes, etc. help you attune to what you already believe, think, and feel, but don't ever allow them to take away your opportunity to make your own choices and decisions. I would also suggest that you make your own predictions, for you are the only one who truly can! *Your answers and your power are always within you.*

### EMPOWERED WOMAN INTUITIVE GUIDANCE PRACTICE

Intuition often comes through in a very compassionate, loving way. If you're trying to tap into your intuition when you feel a lot fear or anxiety and are emotionally triggered about something, begin by grounding and centering yourself. If your mind and emotions are very active, take some deep and slow breaths. You don't have to try to turn off your mind; you just need focus on your heart and use your breath to connect with a quieter, deeper place inside.

You can also bring your attention into your second chakra at the same time so that you are connecting with both of your hearts, as I shared earlier. In this calm, quiet, deeper place beneath all of your thoughts and emotions, you will find your intuition. Place one hand on your heart and the other on your lower belly, your empowered feminine energy center. Breathe deeply and feel your feet on the ground. From this centered place, ask your question and tune in to this deeper part of you, your heart and soul, rather than focusing on the mind chatter and fears in your head. It is here that you will find your accurate, intuitive truth. This can take some practice, but you will soon start to become more and more familiar with your intuition, the voice the voice of your heart and soul.

## THE POWER OF YOUR MIND AND YOUR EMOTIONS

I've emphasized before, the key to manifesting what you want in love and life is working not only with your mind, but also very importantly, with your emotions. You want to be in a high vibrational emotional state as much as possible, even when you don't see your desired results yet in your outer world. Believe me, I know this can challenging. For example, maybe you've been on online dating sites for years, but have yet to meet your man. Or you've been looking for work, but no new job opportunities are showing up. Or perhaps you're doing everything you can to lose weight or heal your body and you haven't seen any positive results. Being an empowered woman usually involves cultivating faith, one of the topics we'll be discussing in chapter seven.

If what you want to manifest is your heart's true desire, it is possible for you to have it in some way, shape or form. Believe in the power you have within and know that there are infinite possibilities out there for you! What you want may not come in the exact way or in the exact form that you wanted, so you need to be open-minded. Be open to miracles because you may end up manifesting something even better than you could possibly imagine!

Look for evidence of possibilities in your outer world. For example, if you are a woman over 50 and you're having a hard time believing it's possible for you to fall in love again, look and ask around, and you may start to hear stories about women over 50, 60, or even 70 who met their true love and even got married later in life. This can then help you to believe that what you want is possible for you as well.

Let's discuss the power of beliefs and emotions further, specifically as they relate to manifesting your desires.

## MANIFESTATION AND YOUR BELIEFS

In chapter three I asked you to think specifically about what it is that you want and then notice if you are telling yourself something about why you can't have it. This will illuminate the limiting beliefs you need to release and reprogram. As I mentioned, you may also need to look at the ways that your subconscious may be trying to protect you. For example, you might have a subconscious fear related to having what you desire.

Let's explore this a little deeper. When my clients are having trouble manifesting what they want, I always ask them the following question, "If you had what you want right now, is there anything about it that might be a problem, or is there anything you might be afraid of?" *When you have difficulty manifesting something, very often it's because you have some subconscious programming that is in conflict with what you consciously want.* **Your subconscious will not allow you to have what you consciously desire if it feels there will be a negative consequence, such as you will be hurt, it won't be safe, or there will be a loss of some kind.**

Here's an example: A client of mine told me that she was not sticking with her healthy diet, even though she really wanted to improve her eating habits. I asked her if she had any fear at all about eating a healthy diet. She thought about it, and then she realized that she was afraid that if she kept eating really healthy while her husband ate his typically unhealthy diet, that they might grow apart. You can see why this fear and belief could prevent her from eating the healthy diet that she and her conscious mind wanted.

***You may need to explore the deeper reasons and fears related to your needs for safety or love in your subconscious mind that are causing you to have difficulty manifesting what you consciously want.*** We all have needs for safety, love, and belonging as we discussed in chapter one. Sometimes our subconscious mind is trying to meet those needs in a way that doesn't serve us anymore, even though it may have helped us to cope with situations in the past. You may need to find a different, healthier way of getting your needs for love or safety met. Or you may need to address possible subconscious blocks to having what you consciously want as we discussed in chapter three, so you can manifest what you want without the conflict and struggle.

For now, if you're having difficulty achieving a goal or manifesting what you consciously want, imagine you already have it. Then go into your heart and see if it feels like a full "Yes, go for it!" or if there is something of which you're afraid. Is there a reason why your subconscious mind might think it's safer for you to not have what you want? Does your subconscious believe you might lose someone's love if you get what you want? You might want to journal about this. When you fear something, there is a part of you that isn't supporting your conscious desire. This creates an *inner conflict* that sounds like, "I want this, but I fear that something negative is going to happen as a result." Or, "If I get what I want, I'm afraid that I may lose something else." Inner conflicts like this create resistance to having what you desire, there is a "I want this, but…" thing going on. For example, you may want a relationship, but you fear losing your freedom. Manifesting is much easier without fear and anticipation of something negative happening if you have what you want.

Another big reason why people have trouble manifesting something is that they don't feel worthy or deserving of it. If this sounds familiar, review the sections in chapter three about increasing your self-esteem and claiming your worthiness. If this sense of unworthiness comes from a mistake you made in the past, review the section about forgiveness in chapter four.

## MANIFESTATION AND YOUR EMOTIONS

In chapter two we discussed the importance of feeling your painful emotions and understanding their messages. This is good and healthy as long as you don't get stuck in or drown in them. Emotions are energy, and they are meant to flow through you. If you stay stuck in them you will be living in the past, and you certainly can't create the future you want from there.

In this chapter you are going to learn how to use the power of uplifting, high vibration emotions to manifest what you want. *It's really the feeling of having what you desire that manifests it.* You must feel like you already have what you want. You must feel the truth of the affirmation, mantra, or new belief in your body and in your heart. Cultivating uplifting high vibrational emotions is what allows your subconscious mind to accept the new true beliefs you've decided to believe instead of the old false ones. *Your subconscious can't accept a new positive thought pattern or true belief if you're feeling terrible emotionally. The uplifting emotion is the carrier of the new thought pattern and belief.*

When you want something in your life, it's because of how you think it will make you feel. Ironically, the ultimate key to manifesting what you desire is to feel the desired feelings now, before you have what you want! Why is this? Because what you're consistently feeling affects your energy and therefore your ability to magnetize to you what you want. If you want to become a more empowered woman, then you need to pay attention to your emotions and notice what you are feeling throughout the day. You need to start cultivating the feelings now that you think you will feel when you have what you desire. *How would you feel right now if you already had what you want?*

*Believe it or not, you actually have the power to feel however you want to feel.* It's not that hard to cultivate a desired feeling. Using the power of your imagination (imagining already having what you desire) and the power of music (listening to music that gives you the feeling of having what you want) are two of the most effective and powerful tools to help you shift into a high vibration emotional state.

*See the Empowered Woman Manifestation Practices coming up soon in this chapter for instructions on how to use these two powerful tools to program your subconscious mind and help you manifest what you want.*

*What can be challenging is to train your mind to keep focusing on those uplifting emotions because very often your limiting beliefs will come up.* Then you may start to feel the painful emotions that go with them if you don't see the evidence of your desired manifestation in your outer world yet. You may notice that you start feel fear, doubt, or hopelessness, for example. You can't be perfect. You're likely going to have some doubt, fear, sadness, or impatience at times when you're in the manifesting process.

Of course, it's okay to feel those painful emotions when they arise, as I will discuss shortly, but you want to be more *consistently* feeling uplifting emotions. For example, let's say you want to find a new home that you love and that you will feel safe and comfortable in. At the end of the day ask yourself, when you thought about your desire for a new home, what was your predominant feeling about it? Were you feeling afraid and hopeless about it most of the day with only a minute or two of feeling the emotions of comfort, safety and excitement? To be able to manifest the healthy love and life you want, your emotions need to be more consistently in a high vibrational state, as if you already had what you desire. *This is being in the energy of wholeness and completeness, rather being in the energy of lack.*

## THE POWER OF YOUR IMAGINATION AND FEELINGS

*Underneath everything is your desire to feel safe, peaceful, loved or happy, and all of these feelings are available inside of you, through your connection to your heart and your Spiritual Source.* As you keep practicing knowing and feeling that what you want is already yours, you are *creating the inner experience* of already having what you desire. You are using the power of your imagination, which is not just visualizing but includes your feelings and emotions.

*When you imagine something, your body and your subconscious mind will respond as if what you're imagining is real and happening now.* For example, if you imagine biting into a lemon and tasting the lemon juice, your mouth will usually start salivating. Both music and your imagination will help you to feel your desired emotions. When you imagine having a loving relationship or a healthier body, the more you will *feel* like you are already in the relationship or that you already have a healthy body now. *See the second Empowered Woman Manifestation Practice below for an explanation and example of how to use your imagination in this way.*

Of course, you don't want to deny painful emotions when they come up. Notice the painful feelings, the fear that you won't be able to have what you want, but at the same time, don't let painful emotions, cause you to buy into the false thought patterns or beliefs that go with them. Say to yourself, "I know you're feeling sad right now, and that sadness is real because that's what you're feeling, but it's not true that you can't have what you want."

***You are not going to believe the false beliefs. And you're not going to keep expecting the same thing to happen in your future.*** Let's say you have a pattern of being rejected in relationships and so you keep expecting more of the same. Instead, when you change and program your subconscious mind with new beliefs and emotions, you'll no longer *expect* to be rejected. *Instead, you'll expect to be loved, wanted, and cherished.* Feel the painful emotions but then as soon as you can, bring yourself back into the higher vibration emotions of joy, gratitude, excitement, peace, love, safety, etc. until you have what you want. Cultivating faith will help you do this, and we'll discuss that in the next chapter. Secrets six and seven are closely related and work together.

## ENJOY THE JOURNEY OF YOUR LIFE

Keep in mind that when you actually do manifest what you want, there will always be something else you want because we are all here to create, grow, expand, and evolve. You don't want to keep postponing your happiness until you have whatever it is that you currently want because then you will never be happy. You'll always be thinking, "I'll be happy when…" Look around in your life now and ask yourself in what ways do you already have what you want or at least the essence of it? ***And most importantly, please remember to feel grateful for what you do have!***

***Try to find enjoyment wherever you are in your life.*** For example, if you're single and working on your own business from home, ask yourself, if you knew that you were going to be in a relationship in a few months, how would you feel about your alone time right now? Would you be enjoying it? Then enjoy it now! Ask yourself, what can you appreciate about where you're at in your life right now before you have what you want? Instead of feeling a sense of lack, see things from the higher perspective of your sixth chakra and trust that everything you are experiencing right now is actually what you need to be experiencing to lead you to what your heart desires.

Let's take your health, for example. If you're having symptoms and you don't now have the healthy body that you want, affirm that your body is moving in the direction of health, recovery, and repair, and believe that your symptoms are a step on the way to good health. Your body is doing what it needs to do to get back into balance. The same goes with relationships. Each person you have been with in the past who didn't work out was teaching you something and leading you to your true love. Each job you have had is guiding you to the ideal work that you love. When you find the beauty, perfection, or blessing where you are now in your life, you will start to feel more love, appreciation, and gratitude, and this will raise your energetic vibration higher, cause your light to shine brighter and brighter, and help you to more easily draw what you want to you.

***In other words, try to see everything that is happening in your life as bringing you closer to what you want, even if it doesn't feel like it right now.*** This is the higher spiritual perspective of your sixth chakra's third eye. It's important to enjoy the journey along the way to what you desire. The journey is empowered feminine energy while empowered masculine energy is about the end result. It's fine to have a goal or a destination, but an important question to ask yourself is whether you are enjoying the journey on the way to your destination. The truth is, if you're not happy on the way to your destination, you won't be happy for very long when you get there! There will simply be something else that you want and you will just keep postponing your happiness.

## MANIFESTATION SUMMARY

To summarize, manifestation involves combining your thoughts, intentions, and vision of what you want with uplifting emotions and feelings. It requires changing your self-concept and identity by *becoming the woman who already has what she desires*. Practice cultivating the state of being that feels like what you want is already yours. Combine the uplifting high vibration emotions of gratitude, love, joy, excitement (and any other feelings you think you'll feel when you have what you want) with your mental intention and vision. Notice any fears or conflicts that come up and work to resolve and reprogram them. Keep creating those new neural pathways we talked about in chapter three and programing uplifting emotions into your subconscious mind to align your energy with what you want. Have patience. Remember, your subconscious mind learns by repetition.

Acknowledge and validate any painful emotions that come up related to your desires but don't believe the false thought patterns and beliefs that go with them. Do your best to consistently stay in high vibration most of the time. Think of yourself as shining your light and being in the flow. Remember how magnetic your heart and empowered feminine energy are and that you don't have to struggle. Be open and receptive and believe that you are right now attracting into your life the perfect people, opportunities, and the support you need to manifest what you want. Hold the belief that you are a woman who can and does manifest what she wants, but surrender and let go of when and how it happens. Trust in divine timing. We'll discuss letting go and divine timing with secret seven.

Here are some empowered woman manifestation practices for you to experiment and have fun with…remember to enjoy the journey on the way to creating what you want!

**EMPOWERED WOMAN MANIFESTATION PRACTICES TO PROGRAM YOUR SUBCONSCIOUS MIND AND CHANGE YOUR ENERGY**

**1 -Listen to music that helps you feel that what you want is already yours. This is one of the most powerful and fun ways to help program your subconscious mind and manifest whatever it is you want!** I've been teaching this practice to my students and clients for years and they have had great fun and success with it. Think of a song which helps you cultivate the feeling you want to feel in your body, in your relationships, or in your life. For example, listen to the beautiful song, "At Last" by Beyonce if you want to attract a loving partner. Or the song, "I Feel Good" by James Brown if you want to improve your health. The song, "Flashdance…What A Feeling" by Irene Cara has always been a favorite of mine to help me overcome my fears and follow my passion in work, life and love. The song, "Respect" by Aretha Franklin is a great tune to increase your feelings of self-confidence. If you can, move your body and dance around as you listen. *The movement will help bring your new feelings deeper into your nervous system and subconscious mind.* Also, if you can dance in front of a mirror and smile, that's even more powerful! This is because your body is your subconscious mind. If you have the app Spotify, you can find just about any song you want! Listen to your chosen songs at least once a day, ideally more if you have time. Choose whatever songs help you to feel the way you want to feel. One woman I know even programmed the ring tone on her phone to play the song, "Flashdance…What A Feeling," by Irene Cara!

**2 -Use the power of your imagination**. When you first wake up in the morning, before you go to sleep at night, or at some other time during the day put some relaxing music or a guided meditation audio on and imagine yourself having what you want. If possible, listen to a meditation with some sound healing music in the background that helps your brain get into the slower theta brainwave state. In this state, your subconscious mind is very open and receptive to change. If you don't have sound healing music that's fine, just breathe, relax, and enjoy using the power of your imagination!

**Imagination example:** Get into a relaxed position either sitting or lying down and close your eyes. First bring to mind a scene of whatever it is that you want, *visualizing* it in as much detail as you can. Next *add feelings* to your visualization. For example, you can imagine cuddling with a loving partner by first visualizing in your mind's eye what you want and then imagining how the cuddling would feel in your body. *Imagine how it would feel* to have this man's loving arms around you, thus creating more of a physical experience since feelings or sensations are in your body. Finally *add your heart and your emotions to the imagery*. What emotions are you feeling as you imagine cuddling with this man? Do you feel love for him? Do you feel his love for you? Do you feel grateful? Do you feel joy in your heart? Are you smiling? Relax, imagine, and enjoy these feelings as long as you like. When you're ready, slowly open your eyes bringing all of the wonderful, pleasant feelings with you. Can you now feel that what you desire is already yours? Do you feel less afraid that you can't or won't have what you want? Are you more relaxed and at peace? If so, this will help you to magnetize your ideal partner to you.

**3 -Pray Rain Journaling** - Instead of just recording your day in a typical journal, write about your feelings as if you have already attracted what you want. For example, "It feels so good to have finally attracted a loving, caring man, or it feels so good to be fitting into my clothes again; I feel so grateful!" In this way, you are describing how you would feel if what you want has already happened.

This technique is called pray rain journaling because of the legend about a tribe of people who prayed for rain when it was desperately needed. They prayed a prayer of gratitude that the rain had already happened, and legend says that rain would always come after they prayed in that way.

Gratitude is very powerful—it's really the highest prayer state there is. When you are in a state of gratitude for something rather than being in the energy of lack, it helps you to feel like what you want is already yours, and that will help you to attract what you want sooner.

**4 -Record your own audio** of mantras or affirmations about what you want to manifest, and listen to it over and over while you exercise, while cooking, in the car, etc. Make sure you are feeling what it would feel like if you had what you want, rather than just listening to or repeating the words. I used this secret when I was looking for a place to live, and I manifested a place that was just what I described on my audio recording. Listen to your recording as often as you can, while feeling high vibration emotions. Remember, your sub-conscious mind learns by repetition.

**5 -Create a vision board with pictures of what you desire or have things around your house that symbolize what it is that you want to manifest.** While writing this book, I kept a piece of paper representing the cover of the book with the title of it on my desk. This helped me to see and feel that the book and my becoming an author was already happening.

To manifest and create what you desire in life, whether you want to lose weight, improve your health, manifest a relationship, find a new home or work that you love, you need to *focus on what you want*, not on what you don't want because *what you focus on will increase*. You don't have to know the whole plan. You can have a vision for what you desire, and it's great to make your visualization as specific as you can. But if it's more of a general vision, that's okay too as long as you have a clear intention, such as, "I desire to have a healthy, loving relationship." Once you have identified your intention, get as clear as you can about what a healthy loving relationship means to you. *Get really clear on how you want to feel with whatever it is you want to create and then every day, take some time to feel those uplifting emotions, tune into your intuition, and ask what the next step is for you.*

## CHAKRA SIX SUMMARY

### How Empowered Woman Secret Number Six Helps You Create the Healthy Love and Life You Want and Deserve

**Health**: Tuning in and listening to your intuition can definitely help you with your health. Your body is communicating to you all the time through physical sensations and symptoms. The physical symptoms are asking for your attention. You can ask your body and your intuition (in whatever way it comes through to you) what it needs or wants and receive guidance that will help you make important health-related decisions. Understanding how manifestation works, using the power of your mind, imagination and emotions, and applying what you learned in this chapter can most definitely improve your health. It can help you to create your ideal body, lose weight, and prevent or even help heal disease.

**Love and Relationships:** Being touch with, listening to and trusting your intuition is essential as far as relationships are concerned. You always want to listen to your gut feelings and pay attention to red flags. When you manifest with your empowered feminine energy and your uplifting emotions you will become more magnetic to true love. When you use the power of your imagination and practice what you learned in this chapter, it will help you create what you desire in love and life. As your inner light gets brighter and stronger because of practicing what you learned with all seven empowered woman secrets, you will be well on your way to making your healthy love and life dreams your new reality!

## CHAKRA SIX EMPOWERED WOMAN MANTRAS

*I am magnetic to my desires.*
*I allow my light shine.*
*My intuition is guiding me.*
*I am in the flow.*
*I am the creative artist of my life.*
*I learn from my life challenges and see my life from a higher perspective.*
*I am committed to my life vision.*
*I trust my intuition.*
*I honor the wise woman in me.*
*I listen to and follow my inner knowing.*
*I program my subconscious mind with positive intentions and uplifting emotions*
*I believe and feel that what I want is on its way to me now.*

# EMPOWERED WOMAN
## SECRET SEVEN

# CHAKRA SEVEN

*Co-Creating Your Life with a Higher Power, Letting Go of*
*Fear-Based Attachment and Cultivating Faith*

# CHAPTER SEVEN
# SECRET SEVEN

The seventh empowered woman secret to creating the healthy love and life you want and deserve corresponds with chakra seven. This chakra is about your relationship with your Spiritual Source. You're not meant to shoulder everything alone. There is a Divine Loving Intelligence to help, support, and guide you. Chakra seven, often called the thousand-petaled lotus, is located just touching the top of your head. Its color is a beautiful purple violet.

## CHAKRA SEVEN - IN YOUR POWER

When you are in your power here, you feel a connection to your soul and have a strong loving relationship with your Spiritual Source. You feel that you are co-creating your life with the Divine. You have a spiritual practice you love and enjoy. You practice acceptance, spiritual surrender, letting go and non-attachment, and this brings you inner peace. You have faith and trust in Divine timing.

## CHAKRA SEVEN - NOT IN YOUR POWER

When you're not in your power in this center, you are more or less closed off to a connection with your soul and a relationship with your Spiritual Source. You may feel like you have to do everything yourself, and it may even seem like you have the weight of the world on your shoulders. You may feel a lack of purpose and meaning in your life. You often get very attached to the specific outcomes you want and have difficulty practicing acceptance and letting go. You tend to be in fear often and try to control everything. It's hard for you to have faith, and it's difficult for you to trust in Divine Timing.

## THE BIG SPIRITUAL PARADOX

The topics of faith and divine timing often bring up the paradox and big question about divine will versus free will. In chapter six and throughout this book, we have discussed the power that you have to create the healthy love and life you want, which sounds very much like free will. Yet I also mentioned that you are co-creating your life with your Divine Source. With this secret, I'm bringing up the concept of divine timing, which sounds like it's related more to a divine will or a divine plan for your life. The question many people ask is whether we have free will or is our life planned out before we get here? Or is it actually both? I will share with you my perspective about how I feel this paradox works from all of my spiritual studies, and then you can see if any part of my philosophy resonates with you.

The way I see it is that you have the freedom to make choices in your life, you have options; you get to choose which direction you go. That is your free will, yet at the same time, there is also a higher power or a divine perspective, which some people call the Universe, Divine Loving Intelligence, God, Goddess, Spiritual Source, etc., and this is the divine will aspect of your life. Our Spiritual Source (the Divine) has a much higher and more expansive perspective than we have as humans.

As a human you have the ability to move from one thing to the next in a linear fashion, but you're not able to see the whole big expanded picture. You're not able to see and know all of the infinite possibilities that might be available to you. You're living day by day, right here and right now, taking things one step at a time.

## THE HIGHER PERSPECTIVE

But from the higher, broader, and more expansive perspective of the Universe, your Spiritual Source sees everything. This Universal Loving Intelligence sees the whole picture. It sees and knows about all of the outcomes and all of the possible paths you could take in your life. If you turn right or left, I believe this Divine All-Knowing Loving Intelligence knows what the outcome will be, where each choice will lead you. Because this Divine Universal

Intelligence is all knowing, it also knows the best path that will get you where you want to go. But because you have free will, you have choices and one of those choices is whether you are going to ask for, listen to, and ultimately follow this Divine Guidance or not.

## DIVINE GUIDANCE

If you decide to follow this divine guidance, then the next question is how does this divine guidance communicate to you? It comes through your heart (the seat of your soul) and your intuition (the voice of your spirit) and your feelings—and these are all aspects of your empowered feminine energy. You don't want to manifest from just your mind and your human personality self (your ego) because yes, they can definitely make something happen, but that doesn't mean it will bring you the happiness you seek. It is your heart and soul that will guide you to true fulfillment in love and life. In other words, *you want to bring your heart and soul and the Divine (your Spiritual Source) into your manifestation process, (that's why it's called co-creation) and you want to align all of your manifesting intentions with love. To me, God is Love—pure, unconditional Divine Love.*

*When you listen to your heart and your intuition, the voice of your soul, and you have a strong connection to your Spiritual Source, you are allowing the Divine to guide you.* You may feel called to do something or go somewhere when something feels right and good to you. Or you may do something that you know is the best thing for you, even though it's not an easy thing to do. In both of these situations, you listen to and follow the deeper wisdom of your heart and soul as you tune in to your connection with your Spiritual Source.

Yes, you always have the free will to choose otherwise, to ignore that voice, your intuition, your heart and divine guidance. Even though your heart's guidance is calling you one way, you can walk the other way. But if you do, you'll usually eventually notice that other way won't feel very good or be very satisfying. Most likely you won't be happy, and the path you have taken won't get you where you really want to go. This is the big paradox. You have free will, and you can choose whatever it is you want to do. But if you really want to be able to be, do, and have what your heart truly desires, then you need to release not only your desire, but also the how, when, and the final outcome of your actions to the Divine Loving Intelligence of the Universe, and allow your Spiritual Source to guide you where it wants you to go, as it communicates with you through your heart and your intuition.

As you take action toward what you want, you allow your Spiritual Source and its Divine Loving Intelligence to take care of the how and the when. You stay open to all possibilities and let go of any fear-based attachment to specific outcomes. More on this shortly. When you let go, very often you are led to something, someone, or somewhere even better than what you originally imagined or wanted. You will often experience synchronicities and miracles along the way. *This will help you strengthen your faith and develop more trust in divine timing.*

## THERE'S NO SUCH THING AS FAILURE

Please remember that if or when doors close, or things don't work out or happen the way you thought they would or wanted them to, it's never because you're not good enough or not worthy. It's the Divine guiding you to go down a different path. Remember what I said at the beginning of the book, yes, you have power, but you are not in full control of everything that happens in your life and all around you. If you are having challenges and don't yet have what you want even though you've been working on things for quite a while, please don't ever start to feel like a failure. *There is no such thing as failure, only opportunities to learn and grow.*

*Trust that whatever pain, adversity, or suffering you are experiencing has a higher purpose for your soul that your human self may not be able to understand.* Allow whatever challenges you are going through to strengthen your relationship with yourself and with your Spiritual Source. Allow them to strengthen your faith and help you to practice spiritual surrender, which is not a giving up, but a letting go. To surrender is to be fully open in a very deep way to each experience rather than judging and resisting whatever is happening or not happening. Surrender is something you do internally while taking the outer needed action and not being attached to the results. It's allowing a greater power and a deeper wisdom to guide you and help you to create your desired life.

## LETTING GO OF FEAR-BASED ATTACHMENT

*There have probably been times when you really wanted something and you were taking all the action you possibly could, but what you wanted was still not happening.* When this is the case, you may start to lose faith and hope and feel like giving up. Trust me, I understand; I've been there. You may become very frustrated and become more and more attached to having whatever it is that you want. You might try to control the outcome of your efforts, even though the outcome is clearly not in your control.

So what is attachment? The kind of attachment we are talking about here is an unhealthy attachment that has a needy, clingy, controlling energy whether it's related to another person or to something else in your life. *This unhealthy attachment is the experience of energetically (emotionally and mentally) holding on to something or someone very tightly and with fear.* In relationships it can feel like you're trying to fill a void, needing someone to do something so you can feel happy or worthy. This, of course, comes from fear.

We discussed fear in general in the first chapter, but here we are going to specifically discuss fear-based attachment to your desires. When you are attached to having something or someone that you want, you are in a state of lack and are afraid that you won't or can't have what you want. Ironically, the more attached and in fear you are about not having or losing what you want, the more you are actually pushing it away from you. Fear is not attractive or magnetic. When I say that an empowered woman knows how to trust, surrender, and let go, I am not asking you to let go of wanting whatever it is that you desire. I am also not telling you to give up—surrender is not giving up; it is accepting the present moment as it is and deeply letting go.

What I am asking you to do is to surrender and let go of the *attachment* to having what you want, in other words, letting go of the fear of not having what you desire. When you do, you will feel at peace. You will then be able to manifest what you want with the energy of love. The opposite of fear, love is a very powerful, attractive, and magnetic energy.

The question you might be asking now is, okay, when your fears come up, how do you let go? You release your fear through your relationship with your Spiritual Source, by placing what you want into the hands of the Divine. Some beautiful release prayers for placing your desires into the hands of the Divine are, "This or something better," "Thy will be done," or "This or whatever is for my highest good and for the highest good of all concerned."

## NON-ATTACHMENT

Non-attachment is wanting what you desire while at the same time *releasing* your desire to your Spiritual Source, *trusting and having faith* that everything is happening exactly as it is meant to be in this moment. In addition, you're not limiting yourself to one specific outcome when the Universe may have something even better in mind for you then exactly what you have envisioned.

***Focus on your desire with love in your heart while at the same time trusting that things are perfect just the way they are right now.*** When you are in the energy of love you don't need to force or control anything; instead, you're allowing things to unfold. You concentrate on the experience you are having, not what the possible outcome of that experience may be. The more you cultivate and strengthen your relationship with your Spiritual Source, the less attached and in fear you will be. If what you want is a true desire of your heart, then do your best to trust and have faith that you will have what you want in some way, in some form, at some time. Know and accept that it may not come in the exact way or form and very often not in the exact timing that you want.

For example, perhaps you really want and feel ready to meet your soulmate, but it's just not happening yet. Perhaps he is not ready yet, but you can't see the big picture or higher perspective the way the Divine Loving Intelligence can. Maybe you want to move, but you can't find the home you're looking for, because the right place for you is not ready yet. This is where your relationship with your Spiritual Source comes in. You very often can't see the reasons why you may not be attracting and manifesting what you want yet. You need to trust and have faith that all is in Divine perfect order, that all is happening as it is meant to for your highest good. ***Quite often, later down the road, you may understand why things happened, didn't happen, or unfolded the way they did.***

Here are some practices to help you let go of attachment.

## EMPOWERED WOMAN PRACTICES FOR RELEASING ATTACHMENT

**1** -Write down what you want to manifest on a piece of paper, fold it up, and place it in a special pretty box or container or inside a spiritual book, something that represents that you are releasing the how and the when of your desired outcome into the hands of your Spiritual Source.

**2** -Accept the moment as it is. Yesterday is gone and tomorrow is yet to come. Be present in the moment and enjoy it as much as you can.

**3** -Notice when, instead of just enjoying your present moment experience, you start to try to control, predict, or manipulate something or begin to fear losing someone or something.

**4** -Remind yourself that you can't change the past. When you hold onto the past, it's often because of fear, fear that you ruined your chances for happiness or fear that you may never know that same happiness again. Instead, focus on what you love in the present moment, and you will create happiness here and now. Make today so meaningful that you don't have time to dwell on yesterday.

**5** -Release the need to know the future and learn to become more comfortable with uncertainty. Don't obsess about tomorrow or wait to be happy because this moment is all there really is. Life will never be perfect, so do what you love now.

**6** -Understand the difference between fear-based attachment and a loving connection with someone. Unhealthy attachment is based in the mind and in fear. You can have fear-based attachments to people and also to outcomes, beliefs, ideas, or thoughts. Fear-based attachment often leads to frustration, heartache, and stress. A loving connection with someone is heart-based and is an accepting and caring exchange of energy between two people. It creates feelings of harmony, peace, compassion and of course more love.

To summarize, you want to manifest from your heart with love, wanting yet at the same time releasing your desires to your Spiritual Source by focusing on your heart and love. Place what you want in the hands of the Divine, perhaps with the release prayers I mentioned earlier or ones that you create on your own.

As you remain open to the magic and mystery of life, sometimes things happen in an even better way than you could have imagined. When challenges or losses happen, see them as opportunities to develop or strengthen your relationship with yourself and with your Spiritual Source. You are being supported by a Divine Loving Intelligence, and you are never truly alone, even though it may feel that way at times. You will be guided and supported. You will start to experience synchronicities that will deepen your faith and increase your trust in divine timing.

## YOUR UNIQUE RELATIONSHIP WITH YOUR SPIRITUAL SOURCE

*Every woman needs to find her own unique way of connecting with her Divine Source.* The most common ways of doing this are with prayer and meditation, but there are other ways such as yoga or spending time in nature. Find the way that feels right and works best for you. I'm guessing that you are like most women who wake up in the morning thinking about everything that you need to do and accomplish. You may go through your day just trying to get it all done. You may tell yourself that you don't have time to pray or meditate. I'm hoping that as you read the rest of this chapter and learn about all of the many benefits of prayer or meditation and how it can help you to become a more empowered woman, that you will create some time to do it.

Connecting with your Spiritual Source helps you to strengthen your *Empowered Woman Within*. If you make it a priority to spend at least five or ten minutes a day connecting with your deeper self (your heart and soul) and your Spiritual Source, you will start to recognize all of the many benefits and will look forward to taking the time to go within. Your relationship with your Divine Source will then be your own.

Some of you may have religious beliefs from childhood that made you feel punished, condemned, or fearful. You need to become aware of and release these old beliefs in order to have a loving relationship with a Spiritual Source. No matter how you were raised, it is your responsibility now to develop your own unique relationship with the Divine. The important thing is that you are consistent in making this relationship a priority, even if it's just for a few minutes a day. Every woman can find a little time every day for this important relationship!

Remember it's your personal connection with your soul and your unique relationship with your Spiritual Source. You get to choose how you spend the time, whether it's praying, meditating, listening to a guided meditation, journaling, reading something inspirational, going for a walk in nature, or practicing yoga. Experiment and find out which activities and practices feel good and work best for you. Start with five or ten minutes and then gradually increase the time as you are able.

Your connection and relationship with your Divine Source will help you along your soul's journey, so create a daily routine, choosing the time or times that are best for you. I find in the morning before starting my day and then again later in the day after work are optimal for me. You'll be surprised at how just a little time connecting with your Spiritual Source helps you receive the guidance, healing, comfort or inspiration that you need.

## MEDITATION

There are many different kinds of prayer and meditation practices that you can explore and choose from. Some of you may practice a formal religion, and prayer is very personal to you, so my focus here will be more general and on meditation. Below is a list of ways meditation helps you to become a more empowered and healthy woman. Most of these benefits apply to prayer as well. You can think of prayer as talking to your Spiritual Source and meditation as more of a tuning in, listening to, and being present with your soul and the Divine.

## BENEFITS OF MEDITATION FOR YOUR EMPOWERED WOMAN WITHIN

**KEY BENEFIT: Meditation helps you to love yourself.** *It a powerful act of self-care and self-love when you take the time to go within to spend time with your own heart and soul and with your Divine Source.*

Below are nine other ways meditation helps you to become a more empowered and healthy woman in your relationships and life.

**1** -It helps you become more aware of your thoughts, beliefs, emotions, habits, and behaviors so that you can then make the changes you want, instead of being run by subconscious programming. Self-awareness is the first step to changing anything.

**2** -It calms your nervous system, which helps you open your heart and be more present to yourself and with others.

**3** -It teaches you to be the observer and helps you learn how to respond from your calm center instead of reacting when you're emotionally triggered.

**4** -It helps you connect with your intuition, gain more clarity, and receive the answers and guidance that you need. It also helps you receive creative ideas and inspiration.

**5** -It helps you to let go of fear in general and fear-based attachment to your desires. It helps you release anxiety and the need to control, to trust the process and go with the flow.

**6** -It helps reduce stress and addictive behaviors, facilitates inner peace and relieves physical pain. Meditation helps you heal your body, improve your health, and enjoy better sleep.

**7** -It brings both your heart and your brain into coherence, a calm, balanced, harmonious state. It helps take your mind off the outer world and your problems and expands your consciousness. It allows you to open your mind and heart and tune into the unified field of Divine Love, receptive to all of the infinite possibilities for you and your life!

**8** -It helps you understand that the ultimate source of the love, peace, and happiness that you seek is actually within you, rather than in the external circumstances of your life. You will be less likely to be caught up in things that are always changing or looking to another person to make you happy. Through your connection to your heart and soul and your relationship with your Divine Source, you will discover a place of joy, love and peace within. You will begin to feel a oneness with all of life and with your Spiritual Source. This feeling of wholeness and unity is love!

**9** -It can help guide and support you through times of change, uncertainty, and transition. I wrote much of this book during the 2020 pandemic, while going through very uncertain times and my own major life transition. I would not have been able to do it without prayer, meditation, and a strong connection to my Spiritual Source!

In a constantly changing and uncertain world, prayer and meditation can help you connect with the part of you that doesn't change. Your thoughts change; your emotions change; your body changes. But deep inside of you there is a part of you that doesn't change—your soul and your connection to Divine Love or the Greater Loving Intelligence of the Universe. When you spend time connecting with this part of you, you will discover that there is a still quiet center within you that is like the eye of a hurricane. You will then be better able to handle and manage the changes and uncertainty in your own life and in the external circumstances and world around you. You can even use the experience of loss, change, and uncertainty to deepen your connection to your Spiritual Source and strengthen your faith.

**DIFFERENT FORMS OF MEDITATION—Cultivating a Personal Relationship with Your Soul and Your Spiritual Source**

*Meditation is about slowing down and becoming more present*. You can simply start your day with the intention of being present that day with whatever you're doing, when you comb your hair, when you brush your teeth, etc. As you focus your mind on each task, keep your attention in the present moment, rather than thinking about the next thing you need to do or place you need to be.

Some of you may already have a meditative or prayer practice that works for you or perhaps you practice a certain religion. Others may be open to exploring prayer or meditation if you don't currently have a practice.

For those of you who are open to exploring, the first suggestion that I have is that you choose a prayer or meditative practice that you enjoy and love to do rather than meditating with the energy of this is something I "should" do. Many women say, "I know I should meditate and I tried it, but I can't do it." What I've discovered is that very often this is because they don't really like or resonate with the kind of meditation they are doing, and that's why it doesn't work for them. It's similar to physical exercise. I teach women to find a form a form of exercise that they really love and enjoy, so they keep up with it and do it. The same applies to your spiritual practice, whether it is some form of prayer, meditation, or something else like spending time in nature. *Find something that you enjoy and that feels good to you!*

*Every woman is unique, and sometimes you need to experiment with different things until you find what works for you. You don't have to practice just one kind of meditation each day.* I do a specific kind of prayer and meditation practice in the morning and then later on in the afternoon, I listen to a guided meditation, and it may not be the same guided meditation every day. You can have a variety of meditations in your tool kit or on your iPod or phone and tune in to yourself daily to see what kind of prayer or meditation you need on that particular day. Ask yourself what would feel good and best to you? Many of my clients love to listen to guided meditations and find them very effective and helpful, especially with sound healing music in the background. I have recorded many of these, including the free *Empowered Woman Within* guided meditation that is a companion to this book!

**Here are a few of the many different forms of meditation. Find the ones that you resonate with and enjoy.**

**Focused Awareness Meditations**. Almost all meditation involves some kind of focus, whether it's focusing on your breath or on a mantra, which is a powerful affirmation that carries a high vibration. In this type of meditation, every time your mind wanders, you simply bring it back to your breath or the mantra.

**Guided meditations**. In this recorded form, someone is guiding you to imagine or feel a certain way. These can also include powerful mantras to program your subconscious mind and relaxing, sound healing music in the background.

**Mindfulness Meditation.** In this practice, instead of focusing on just one thing, you mindfully observe everything that is happening. You notice with acceptance your physical sensations, your thoughts, and any emotions that you feel as they arise. You focus your awareness on the present moment while calmly acknowledging and accepting your feelings, thoughts, and bodily sensations.

**Loving Kindness Meditation/Prayer Practice.** This involves repeating silently or out loud prayer statements such as, "May I be at peace. May my loved ones be at peace. May the world be at peace. May I be healed, etc."

**Sound Healing Music Meditations**. These are music recordings with special rhythms called binaural beats that help slow down your brainwaves and move you into a relaxed body-mind state. As your brainwaves slow down into the theta brainwave state and you become more relaxed, you can more easily connect with your deeper self and with your Spiritual Source. Your subconscious mind will also be very open and receptive to the spoken words, images and feelings. I use this kind of music on my guided meditation audios.

**Energy Clearing and Energy Healing Kinds of Meditations.** In this type of guided meditation, you work with your chakras and your aura using your imagination and possibly colors. Grounding meditations, where you imagine connecting with the earth in various ways as we discussed with secret one, would also fall into this category.

**Moving Meditation.** Yoga, tai chi, and walking meditations fall into this category. Walking a labyrinth is also a moving meditation. Moving meditation may appeal to people who have difficulty sitting and quieting their minds.

**Heart Connection Meditation**. I teach and practice a method of meditation that I call Heart Connection Meditation. To me your heart is the most powerful place for you to focus during prayer and meditation. Remember, your heart is the bridge between your human self and your divine self.

In this practice you first bring your attention into your heart center and then you *feel into your heart.* This gives you a sense of connecting with the Divine, of connecting with love. As you feel the energy of love in your heart, you will start to relax and feel more at peace. ***If you notice that your mind is wandering, bring it back to your heart, back to that felt experience of love.***

Your heart is where you can connect with your soul, and your soul is always connected to a very powerful Divine Loving Energy and Intelligence. The more you connect with your heart and feel the presence of this Divine Love, the more self-love you will feel and the more loving you will be with others. The more you will be in your empowered energies, especially your empowered feminine energy, rather than being in disempowered, needy, codependent energy.

## THE POWER OF YOUR SOUL AND YOUR HIGHER AWARENESS

Whatever form or forms of prayer and meditation you practice, you will be strengthening your connection and relationship with your Spiritual Source. You're connecting to the deeper part of you that is always one with the Divine. You will not only feel a sense of peace and love, but you also will start to realize how powerful you really are. You will discover that you are more than your body, more than your thoughts, more than your emotions—you are a soul or a spirit that has a body, that has thoughts, that experiences emotions. As a soul or spirit, you can observe those things about yourself, your physical sensations, your emotions and your thoughts.

*When you are connected to the part of you that can observe all of these different parts of yourself with your higher awareness, you are in your power. You can then change whatever you want to change, such as unhealthy, disempowering relationship patterns, how you communicate, how you handle your emotions, or how you feel about yourself and your body.*

The more you take some time to go within and give attention to your two important internal relationships—your relationship with yourself and your relationship with your Spiritual Source—the more benefits and happiness you will experience in your relationships and in your life.

## NON-ATTACHMENT AND HAPPINESS

Earlier in this chapter, I mentioned that one of the wonderful benefits of developing and strengthening a relationship with your Spiritual Source is that it helps you become less attached to having what you want, which paradoxically allows you to manifest what you want sooner or easier. Please keep in mind that I am not talking about being *detached* or that you don't care anymore. You are also not giving up.

*When you are non-attached, you're still caring and wanting what you want but at the same time you're releasing your attachment to your desired outcome and your fear of not having it. The difference between surrender and giving up is having faith. When you give up you feel hopeless and possibly depressed. When you surrender your desire you give it to your Spiritual Source. You place it in the hands of the Divine and you feel at peace. You release your fear, you let go and trust that higher divine loving forces are at play in your life - you have faith.*

Remember, attachment is the experience of energetically (emotionally and mentally) holding onto something or someone very tightly, because you think and feel you need it to feel good, to be happy, or to feel peaceful and secure. Attachment is an energetic state of lack within yourself caused by thinking something outside of you is the key to your happiness.

This feeling of lack within is the experience of not having what you want and it will often just keep creating more of the same. When you strengthen your relationship with your Spiritual Source, you will feel happier within yourself and more accepting of the present moment which will bring you inner peace.

In contrast, when you're attached and in fear, deep down you're always feeling that somehow you're not okay, safe, or loved and that you'll be happy "when." You have the feeling that *something is always missing* and that this present moment is somehow not acceptable or good enough. You keep telling yourself that changing a life circumstance or something about your partner or that having a partner will give you the peace, calm, security, love or happiness that you want, but you eventually realize that you can't get it outside of yourself in a way that lasts. ***The truth is, happiness doesn't have to depend on specific outer conditions and circumstances. You can actually create it for yourself on the inside and then like a powerful magnet you allow your outer circumstances to become a match to it.***

In order to release attachment and create what your heart desires, you not only need to cultivate the *inner experience* of already having what you want, as you learned with secret six, but you also need to nurture the feeling of being *okay, happy, or at peace as you are and where you are right now.* I'm not saying that you have to like whatever you're currently experiencing; I'm simply saying that you can learn to accept what is rather than resisting it and creating more stress for yourself. Acceptance is actually the first step to changing something.

When you let go, accept, and feel that everything is as it is meant to be in this particular moment, you naturally start to realize that the essence of what you want, which is peace, love, and happiness, is available to you within your own heart. ***You realize that inside your heart, beneath all of your ever-changing emotions, thoughts, and life circumstances, there is a steady, calm, peaceful, and unconditionally loving presence and energy.***

***Tapping into and focusing on the love energy and peace inside your own heart will bring you happiness and will help you feel like a self-confident, empowered woman who already has what she desires. It's a very attractive and deep internal state of being.***

If instead you are attached and in fear, you will often feel like you can't be happy until you have what you want. You're always waiting…waiting for someone or something outside of you to make you happy. This is giving your power away. As an empowered woman you understand that you have the power to be happy now, and you have the power to feel the way you want to feel right now. You may not like what is happening or not happening in your life at the moment, but you are not in a state of resistance to it. *You're not waiting to be happy because you know you can be happy now. You're not waiting to be loved because you know that you can feel love in any given moment, because you are always connected to love.*

## YOU ARE ALWAYS CONNECTED TO LOVE

You're always connected to your Spiritual Source, therefore you are always connected to love. It's very easy to forget this at times and feel like you are lacking something, that something is missing, or that you are unloved or separate from love and your Spiritual Source. Feeling anxious, lonely, hopeless, or unhappy are signs that you may be feeling separate and that you need to connect with your Spiritual Source. You are always connected to a Divine Loving Energy—you always have been and you always will be. You are made of this loving energy, and you are one with Divine Love, therefore you can never be separate from it. The more you tap into and feel this love within your heart, the happier and more at peace you will be and the more faith you will have that all is in Divine Perfect Order, no matter how things may appear in your outer world at the time.

*You will begin to feel that nothing is missing in this present moment, yet at the same time you also realize and know that nothing is off limits, meaning that all things are possible! You know that happiness arises when you are your authentic self, true to your own heart and soul.*

*As you follow your heart and soul's true yearnings, you will be guided and supported by your Spiritual Source and you will strengthen your Empowered Woman Within. You will be well on your way to creating the healthy love and life that you've always wanted and very much deserve!*

**CHAKRA SEVEN SUMMARY**

**How Secret Number Seven Helps You Create the Healthy Love and Life You Want and Deserve**

**Health:** When you let go of fear-based attachment to your desired outcomes, you will be at peace. Inner peace is vitally important for your physical health. Getting into slower meditative brainwave states on a consistent basis, in whatever way you choose, is also beneficial for your health. It strengthens your immune system, calms your nervous system, helps you cope better with stress, and brings your body back into a calm body-mind state after challenging situations. Cultivating a strong consistent relationship with your Spiritual Source helps you release fear and focus on love—and ultimately, love is what heals you and your body.

**Love and relationships:** When you let go of fear-based attachment to your desired outcome, you can trust, have faith and allow things to unfold naturally. Instead of trying to control what happens, which comes from fear, you will be more present and aware of what is actually happening (or not happening) in your relationships. This helps you decide if you want to continue or end a relationship, to know how much of your emotional energy you want to invest if you're dating, to not fall in love with a man's potential, but to really see him for who he is and how he is showing up (or not showing up) for you now.

Practicing meditation and mindfulness helps you be the observer in your relationships and to respond instead of react. It also helps you become more aware of your thoughts, beliefs, emotions, habits, and patterns. Self-awareness is the first step and the key to changing anything you want to change about yourself and in your interactions with others.

When you recognize that you are co-creating your life with a Divine Loving Intelligence and Higher Power, when you connect with your heart and soul and cultivate a consistent relationship with your Divine Source, you will feel loved, guided, safe, and supported and you will know that you are never alone. You will stop making your partner or potential partners your Source, which means you will stop giving your power away. You will realize that everything you seek, love, health, happiness, and peace comes from within, through your connection to your own heart and soul and your relationship with your Spiritual Source. With that understanding you will no longer settle or stay too long in unhealthy or unfulfilling relationships. You will begin creating the healthy love and life you truly want and deserve!

## CHAKRA SEVEN EMPOWERED WOMAN MANTRAS

*I have a strong relationship with my Spiritual Source.*

*I release fear-based attachments to my desired outcomes.*

*I surrender and let go.*

*I place my desires in the hands of the Divine.*

*I trust and have faith in Divine timing.*

*I have a spiritual practice that I love and enjoy.*

*I know that everything happening in my life right now is in Divine Perfect Order.*

*I am true to my heart and soul.*

*The love of my Spiritual Source surrounds me, protects me and guides me.*

*I know that nothing is missing within me and that all things are possible.*

*I choose love and happiness now.*

*I am co-creating a life that I love with my Divine Source.*

# BRIEF SUMMARY AND
# FINAL WORDS

**WHEN YOU STAY CONNECTED TO YOUR EMPOWERED WOMAN WITHIN**

IN CHAKRA ONE - You are grounded and feel supported. You trust yourself and life. You let go and release unhealthy fears. You feel a sense of safety and security within yourself. You are present in and take good care of your body and your health. You unconditionally love your body. You live in the present moment. You have an abundance consciousness.

IN CHAKRA TWO - You embrace your empowered feminine energy and support it with your empowered masculine energy. You are emotionally present to yourself and then to others. You are the master of your emotions. You express how you feel and ask for what you need and want. You enjoy both your sensuality and sexuality. You are receptive. You are creative. You love being a woman.

IN CHAKRA THREE - You have self-confidence. You feel worthy. You have high self-esteem and healthy boundaries and standards. You release and reprogram false, limiting beliefs and subconscious programming that no longer serves you. You release and change disempowering relationship patterns. You believe in yourself. You feel powerful. You claim your worthiness from within.

IN CHAKRA FOUR - You allow yourself to be both strong and vulnerable. Your heart is open. You let go of the past. You forgive yourself and others. You have a loving relationship with yourself. You are curious, kind, and compassionate. You feel lovable just as you are. You love yourself and others unconditionally. You radiate love. You listen to and follow your heart's deepest yearnings. You are grateful. You are able to give and receive an abundance of love.

IN CHAKRA FIVE - You embrace your healthy vulnerability. You allow yourself to be seen, heard, and known. You practice assertiveness, empowered loving communication, and speaking your truth with love. Your communication brings you closer to those that you love and care about.

IN CHAKRA SIX - You have a beautiful vision for your life. You trust and follow your intuition. You manifest what you want with your intuition, imagination and empowered feminine energy. You learn and grow through your love and life challenges and overcome adversity. You see your life from the higher perspective of your soul. You allow your light to shine.

IN CHAKRA SEVEN - You let go of control and release fear-based attachment. You surrender and let go. You have faith. You allow things to unfold. You stop waiting to feel loved. You stop waiting to be happy. You choose love and happiness now. You recognize that the source of the peace, love and happiness that you seek is within you. You trust in divine timing. You co-create a life that you love with your Spiritual Source.

As you awaken and embrace your *Empowered Woman Within* you let go of trying to change, control or fix other people and situations that you have no power over.

You let go of feeling that other people or situations have power over you.

Instead, you love and empower yourself from within, feeling and owning the power that you have to change yourself and your life.

You know that your power is always within and that your greatest power is love, starting with self-love and Divine Love.

You stop settling in your relationships and in your life because you love yourself and know that you are worthy of all that your heart desires!

Like a rare diamond, you know that you are a uniquely beautiful, multi-faceted, divine embodiment of love and light.

*You know that you are the creative artist of your precious life, and that you are a woman who has the power to manifest the healthy love and life that you truly want - and deserve!*

So what are you waiting for? Life is short and sweet.

You now know the *Secrets of the Empowered Woman.*

*May you radiate empowered love and light in all seven of your chakras, and enjoy the journey on the way to creating your healthy love and life dreams!*

Thank you for taking this incredible journey with me through your seven chakras.

*Know that your Empowered Woman Within is always with you - inside your own body, mind, heart and soul - ready and waiting for you to awaken, embrace and embody her… in all of your relationships and in every aspect of your life!*

I wish you so much love and many healing blessings!

–Sophia Rose

*"Life is what you make it! It's up to you to make yourself happy!"*

–Dorothy C. Gresto

Wise words indeed Mom, wise words indeed. I hope this book has made you smile and that I have made you proud.

# EMPOWERED WOMAN PRAYER

Empowered feminine energy, the power of love is rising
Mothers, daughters, sisters, let us all join together and radiate love and light
May we come to know our divine true nature, learn how to love ourselves
and be the authentic, empowered women we were born and meant to be
May the power of love, starting with self-love, heal and transform us all
As we follow our heart's desires, may we heal and transform our world

Beautiful empowered woman, *it's time to let your light shine.*

~ Sophia Rose

# THE LOVE HEALS METHOD COACHING PHILOSOPHY

The state of a woman's physical, emotional, mental, and spiritual health are all interconnected.

The state of a woman's health, relationships and life are interconnected.

You are a powerful woman.

Your power is within.

Your greatest power is love, starting with self-love and Divine Love.

You are worthy and lovable just as you are.

You are innately worthy of all that your heart desires.

You have the power to create the healthy love and life you want and deserve.

# THE EMPOWERED WOMAN WITHIN GUIDED MEDITATION

**To reinforce what you've learned be sure to download,** *The Empowered Woman Within* **guided meditation companion to this book!** This is a relaxing and uplifting 35-minute guided meditation journey through your chakras, first to clear energy blockages then to program your subconscious mind with new healing and empowering feelings, beliefs and behavior patterns. Beautiful background music with sound healing binaural beats to facilitate deep receptivity to the spoken words. Listen with headphones for deep relaxation and body-mind-spirit transformation or play in the background for continued programming and inspiration while you walk, exercise or practice yoga. Excellent to listen to before sleep, before a date, before an important meeting or event, or whenever you want to increase your self-confidence and self-esteem as well as your inner glow, radiance and attractiveness.

To receive and download your free *Empowered Woman Within* guided meditation companion to this book visit: www.TheLoveHealsMethod.com/pages/free

**For individual support and information about virtual coaching with me, please visit the coaching page on my website:**

### TheLoveHealsMethod.com

# ABOUT THE AUTHOR

Sophia Rose is a Master Certified Healthy Love and Life Coach, Spiritual Coach, teacher, speaker, and author. For the past 20 years she has been an inspirational teacher, transformational coach and women's empowerment expert serving thousands of women around the country. Sophia taught and coached for 15 years at the internationally known Optimum Health Institute of San Diego, a holistic health and wellness spiritual retreat center, and at Vera Via, a five-star health and wellness resort center in Carlsbad, California, voted one of the top five best places in the world for mind-body rejuvenation by the *Wall Street Journal*. She currently speaks and teaches workshops both in person and virtually for various women's groups and organizations, yoga studios, bookstores, health resorts, body-mind-spirit businesses, and wellness centers.

Sophia provides virtual healthy love and life coaching and spiritual coaching for women throughout the country using her unique and holistic *Empowered Woman Within* coaching process, *The Love Heals Method*. She is the creator of two downloadable audio courses, *The Empowered Woman* and *How to Stay Healthy, Strong and Powerful in Body, Mind, Heart and Spirit*. With her calm, soothing voice, she has recorded over 25 downloadable guided meditations. Sophia lives in the beautiful North County area of San Diego, California. She may be contacted through her website at: www.TheLoveHealsMethod.com

ISBN 978-0-578-36114-7

51495

9 780578 361147